THE PENGUIN SHAKESPEARE
EDITED FROM THE ORIGINAL TEXT
BY G. B. HARRISON
18
THE SONNETS

WILLIAM SHAKESPEARE
THE SONNETS
AND
A LOVER'S COMPLAINT

PENGUIN BOOKS

HARMONDSWORTH · MIDDLESEX

ENGLAND

THIS EDITION FIRST PUBLISHED 1938
REVISED AND REPRINTED 1949

THE PORTRAIT
ON THE COVER AND ON THE TITLE
WAS ENGRAVED IN WOOD
FOR THIS EDITION BY
REYNOLDS STONE

MADE AND PRINTED IN GREAT BRITAIN
BY WYMAN AND SONS, LIMITED,
LONDON, FAKENHAM AND READING

WILLIAM SHAKESPEARE

William Shakespeare was born at Stratford upon Avon in April, 1564. He was the third child, and eldest son, of John Shakespeare and Mary Arden. His father was one of the most prosperous men of Stratford who held in turn the chief offices in the town. His mother was of gentle birth, the daughter of Robert Arden of Wilmcote. In December, 1582, Shakespeare married Ann Hathaway, daughter of a farmer of Shottery, near Stratford; their first child Susanna was baptized on May 6, 1583, and twins, Hamnet and Judith, on February 22, 1585. Little is known of Shakespeare's early life; but it is unlikely that a writer who dramatized such an incomparable range and variety of human kinds and experiences should have spent his early manhood entirely in placid pursuits in a country town. There is one tradition, not universally accepted, that he fled from Stratford because he was in trouble for deer stealing, and had fallen foul of Sir Thomas Lucy, the local magnate; another that he was for some time a schoolmaster.

From 1592 onwards the records are much fuller. In March, 1592, the Lord Strange's players produced a new play at the Rose Theatre called *Harry the Sixth*, which was very successful, and was probably the *First Part of Henry VI*. In the autumn of 1592 Robert Greene, the best known of the professional writers, as he was dying wrote a letter to three fellow writers in which he warned them against the ingratitude of players in general, and in particular against an 'upstart crow' who 'supposes he is as much able to bombast out a blank verse as the best of you: and being an absolute Johannes Factotum is in his own conceit the only Shake-scene in a country.' This is the first reference to Shakespeare, and the whole passage suggests that Shakespeare had become suddenly famous as a playwright. At this time Shakespeare was brought into touch with Edward Alleyne the great tragedian, and Christopher Marlowe, whose thundering parts of Tamburlaine, the Jew of Malta and Dr Faustus Alleyne was acting, as well as Hieronimo, the hero of Kyd's *Spanish Tragedy*, the most famous of all Elizabethan plays.

In April, 1593, Shakespeare published his poem *Venus and Adonis*, which was dedicated to the young Earl of Southampton: it was a great and lasting success, and was reprinted nine times in the next few years. In May, 1594, his second poem, *The Rape of Lucrece*, was also dedicated to Southampton.

There was little playing in 1593, for the theatres were shut during a severe outbreak of the plague; but in the autumn of 1594, when the plague ceased, the playing companies were re-organized, and Shakespeare became a sharer in the Lord Chamberlain's company who went to play in the Theatre in Shoreditch. During these months Marlowe and Kyd had died. Shakespeare was thus for a time without a rival. He had already written the three parts of *Henry VI, Richard III, Titus Andronicus, Two Gentlemen of Verona, Love's Labour's Lost, The Comedy of Errors*, and *The Taming of the Shrew*. Soon afterwards he wrote the first of his greater plays – *Romeo and Juliet* – and he followed this success in the next three years with *A Midsummer Night's Dream, Richard II*, and *The Merchant of Venice*. The two parts of *Henry IV*, introducing Falstaff, the most popular of all his comic characters, were written in 1597-8.

The company left the Theatre in 1597 owing to disputes over a renewal of the ground lease, and went to play at the Curtain in the same neighbourhood. The disputes continued throughout 1598, and at Christmas the players settled the matter by demolishing the old Theatre and re-erecting a new playhouse on the South bank of the Thames, near Southwark Cathedral. This playhouse was named the Globe. The expenses of the new building were shared by the chief members of the Company, including Shakespeare, who was now a man of some means. In 1596 he had bought New Place, a large house in the centre of Stratford, for £60, and through his father purchased a coat-of-arms from the Heralds, which was the official recognition that he and his family were gentlefolk.

By the summer of 1598 Shakespeare was recognized as the greatest of English dramatists. Booksellers were printing his more popular plays, at times even in pirated or stolen version, and he received a remarkable tribute from a young writer named Francis Meres, in his book *Palladis Tamia*. In a long catalogue of English authors Meres gave Shakespeare more prominence than any other writer, and mentioned by name twelve of his plays.

Shortly before the Globe was opened, Shakespeare had completed the cycle of plays dealing with the whole story of the Wars of the Roses with *Henry V*. It was followed by *As You Like it*, and *Julius Caesar*, the first of the maturer tragedies. In the next three years he wrote *Troilus and Cressida*, *The Merry Wives of Windsor*, *Hamlet* and *Twelfth Night*.

On March 24, 1603, Queen Elizabeth died. The company had often performed before her, but they found her successor a far more enthusiastic patron. One of the first acts of King James was to take over the company and to promote them to be his own servants, so that henceforward they were known as the King's Men. They acted now very frequently at Court, and prospered accordingly. In the early years of the reign Shakespeare wrote the more sombre comedies, *All's Well that Ends Well*, and *Measure for Measure*, which were followed by *Othello*, *Macbeth* and *King Lear*. Then he returned to Roman themes with *Antony and Cleopatra* and *Coriolanus*.

Since 1601 Shakespeare had been writing less, and there were now a number of rival dramatists who were introducing new styles of drama, particularly Ben Jonson (whose first successful comedy, *Every Man in his Humour*, was acted by Shakespeare's company in 1598), Chapman, Dekker, Marston, and Beaumont and Fletcher who began to write in 1607. In 1608 the King's Men acquired a second playhouse, an indoor private theatre in the fashionable quarter of the Blackfriars. At private theatres, plays were performed indoors; the prices charged were higher than in the public playhouses, and the audience consequently was more select. Shakespeare seems to have retired from the stage about this time: his name does not occur in the various lists of players after 1607. Henceforward he lived for the most part at Stratford where he was regarded as one of the most important citizens. He still wrote a few plays, and he tried his hand at the new form of tragi-comedy – a play with tragic incidents but a happy ending – which Beaumont and Fletcher had popularized. He wrote four of these – *Pericles*, *Cymbeline*, *The Winter's Tale* and *The Tempest*, which was acted at Court in 1611. For the last four years of his life he lived in retirement. His son Hamnet had died in 1596: his two daughters were now married. Shakespeare died at Stratford upon Avon on April 23, 1616, and was buried in the chancel of the church, before the high altar. Shortly afterwards a memorial which still exists, with a portrait bust, was set up on the North wall. His wife survived him.

*

THE WORKS OF SHAKESPEARE

APPROXIMATE DATE	PLAYS	FIRST PRINTED
Before 1594	HENRY VI *three parts*	Folio 1623
	RICHARD III	1597
	TITUS ANDRONICUS	1594
	LOVE'S LABOUR'S LOST	1598
	THE TWO GENTLEMEN OF VERONA	Folio
	THE COMEDY OF ERRORS	Folio
	THE TAMING OF THE SHREW	Folio
1594–1597	ROMEO AND JULIET (*pirated* 1597)	1599
	A MIDSUMMER NIGHT'S DREAM	1600
	RICHARD II	1597
	KING JOHN	Folio
	THE MERCHANT OF VENICE	1600
1597–1600	HENRY IV *part i*	1598
	HENRY IV *part ii*	1600
	HENRY V (*pirated* 1600)	Folio
	MUCH ADO ABOUT NOTHING	1600
	MERRY WIVES OF WINDSOR (*pirated* 1602)	Folio
	AS YOU LIKE IT	Folio
	JULIUS CÆSAR	Folio
	TROYLUS AND CRESSIDA	1609
1601–1608	HAMLET (*pirated* 1603)	1604
	TWELFTH NIGHT	Folio
	MEASURE FOR MEASURE	Folio
	ALL'S WELL THAT ENDS WELL	Folio
	OTHELLO	1622
	LEAR	1608
	MACBETH	Folio
	TIMON OF ATHENS	Folio
	ANTONY AND CLEOPATRA	Folio
	CORIOLANUS	Folio
After 1608	PERICLES (*omitted from the Folio*)	1609
	CYMBELINE	Folio
	THE WINTER'S TALE	Folio
	THE TEMPEST	Folio
	HENRY VIII	Folio

POEMS

VENUS AND ADONIS	1593
THE RAPE OF LUCRECE	1594
SONNETS A LOVER'S COMPLAINT }	1609
THE PHŒNIX AND THE TURTLE	1601

SHAKESPEARE'S SONNETS

I

On the 20th May 1609 Thomas Thorpe entered in the Stationers' Register, and so acquired sole right to print, 'a Booke called Shakespeares sonnettes.' The book was on sale soon after, for on the back of a letter dated 19th June 1609 Edward Alleyne, the actor, in jotting down a list of purchases, included 'Shakspers Sonnets 5d'. Thorpe's quarto has the title-page:

SHAKE-SPEARES
SONNETS.

Neuer before Imprinted.

AT LONDON

By G. *Eld* for T.T. and are
to be solde by *Iohn Wright, dwelling*
at Christ Church gate.
1609.

Thorpe dedicated the volume in a curious and enigmatic dedication (reproduced on p. 24): TO. THE. ONLIE. BE-GETTER. OF. THESE. INSVING. SONNETS. MR. W. H.

Some at least of the Sonnets were more than ten years old by 1609. Francis Meres, in his book *Palladis Tamia*, printed in 1598, wrote of Shakespeare's poetry: 'As the soul of Euphorbus was thought to live in Pythagoras: so the sweet witty soul of Ovid lives in mellifluous and honey-tongued Shakespeare, witness his *Venus and Adonis*, his *Lucrece*, his sugared Sonnets among his private friends, &c.'

In 1599 William Jaggard the printer issued a little book entitled 'The Passionate Pilgrime. By W. Shakespeare'. It

contains twenty short poems. Nos. 1 and 2 are versions of
Sonnets 138 and 144. Nos. 3, 5, 17 are poems taken from
Shakespeare's play *Love's Labour's Lost*. Of the rest No. 8
is by Richard Barnefield, No. 11 by Bartholomew Griffin,
No. 12 probably by Thomas Deloney, No. 20 prints in-
complete Marlowe's 'Come live with me and be my love'.
Nos. 7, 9, 10, 13–16, 18, 19 are not otherwise known.

A third edition of *The Passionate Pilgrime* was issued in
1612 'Wherewith is newly added two Love Epistles, the
first from Paris to Helen, and Helen's answer back again
to Paris'. These Epistles were not written by Shakespeare,
but were taken from *Troia Britannica* by Thomas Heywood.
Heywood was annoyed and protested in the Epistle to the
Printer in his *Apology for Actors* (1612):

'Here likewise, I must necessarily insert a manifest
injury done me in that work, by taking the two Epistles
of Paris to Helen, and Helen to Paris, and printing them
in a less volume, under the name of another, which
may put the world in opinion I might steal them from
him; and he to do himself right, hath since published
them in his own name: but as I must acknowledge my
lines not worthy his patronage, under whom he hath
published them, so the Author I know much offended
with Mr. Jaggard that (altogether unknown to him)
presumed to make so bold with his name.'

From these words it appears that the *Sonnets* were
published with Shakespeare's approval.

II

Shakespeare's Sonnets are the most disputed of all col-
lections of poetry in the English language. This is not sur-
prising, for they are personal and intimate poems written
to individuals, which would tell much of Shakespeare's

life if only some facts about them could be indisputably established. As it is, neither the date of their writing, nor the persons, have been certainly identified, and critics will continue to argue until some new records come to light.

There are in all a hundred and fifty-four sonnets. As arranged in Thorpe's edition they tell a story. Sonnets 1 to 17 form a series addressed to a beautiful youth, invoking him to marry and so preserve the type in a child, or preferably (Sonnet 6) in ten children. From Sonnet 18 to Sonnet 126 the poet addresses the youth on different topics and occasions, and in changing moods. The sense of intimacy increases; admiration warms into love. The youth is of surpassing and effeminate beauty (18 to 20). At first the poet is shy and tongue-tied in his presence, and can only express himself in writing (23). The poet is separated by travel, but thinks continuously of the youth (27). He is an outcast, but comforted by the thought of his love (29). He warns his friend not to honour him publicly, lest he become tainted with scandal (36). The friend steals the poet's mistress, but is forgiven (40-2). The poet has the youth's picture which he wears at his breast on a journey (47-9). The poet is elderly (73). He is jealous because others seek the youth's patronage, especially one poet whose verse bears 'proud full sail' (78-86). The poet gently rebukes the youth for wantonness (96). After a spring and a summer's separation the poet comes back to his friend (97-8). The poet congratulates the youth on his escape from a 'confin'd doom' (107). He is reconciled after absence (109). He is disgusted with the stigma of his profession (110-11). He defends himself against the charge of ingratitude (117). He apologizes for giving away the 'tables' which the youth had given him (122).

The series to the youth ends with Sonnet 126. Sonnets

127 to 152 are addressed to a Dark Lady, or, as the poet more bluntly calls her, a Black Woman, who is skilled in playing on the virginals, who is faithless, wanton, physically unattractive, false to her bed-vow, and yet irresistibly desirable.

The collection ends with two conventional love-sonnets on Cupid (153, 154).

A personal story, so fragmentary and yet so intimate, is not likely to have left a trace, except by a lucky accident, in any kind of record.

III

The problems of the Sonnets are, therefore, considerable. In any convincing solution it is necessary first of all to identify the youth, and to answer the following questions:

(1) The Sonnets are dedicated to 'Mr W. H.' Who was this 'Mr W. H.'?

(2) Most of the Sonnets are written to a beautiful young man. Was he 'Mr W. H.'? If not, who was he?

(3) In Sonnets 1 to 17 the young man is urged to marry. Is there any evidence that the young man was reluctant to marry?

(4) What external evidence connects him with Shakespeare?

(5) Who was the rival poet of Sonnet 86?

(6) Who was the mistress whom the youth stole?

(7) Who was the Black Woman?

(8) To what events, national and personal, does Sonnet 107 refer?

(9) Are the Sonnets in their right order?

(10) Do they tell a consistent story, and, if so, does this story tally with the known facts of the lives of Shakespeare and the youth?

(11) When were the Sonnets written?

An attempt to answer Questions 1–4, 10–11 can now be made. The other questions are dealt with in the Notes on the particular Sonnets.

Question 9 cannot be definitely answered. Some of the Sonnets are obviously grouped in a logical order, e.g. 1–17, 127–152. Moreover if Shakespeare (as Heywood implies) was responsible for their publication, he approved of the order. It is better to leave them as they stand than to attempt any fancy re-arrangement even though the sequence is not always chronological.

IV

It seems clear from Sonnet 104 that the Sonnets cover a period of more than three years.

The vogue of the Elizabethan Sonnet was short-lived. Although a few poets had written sonnets before 1590, the posthumous publication of Sir Philip Sidney's *Astrophel and Stella* (which told the story of his love for Penelope, Lady Rich) in the spring of 1591 started a new fashion. Anything written by Sidney was eagerly read, and his series of sonnets was at times so personal and sincere that it revealed possibilities hitherto unrealized by English poets. In 1592 appeared Samuel Daniel's *Delia*: in 1593 Thomas Watson's *Tears of Fancy*, Barnabe Barnes' *Parthenophil and Parthenope*, Thomas Lodge's *Phyllis* and Giles Fletcher's *Lycia*: in 1594 Henry Constable's *Diana*, the anonymous *Zepheria*, William Percy's *Sonnets to Caelia*, Michael Drayton's *Idea's Mirror*: in 1595 Edmund Spenser's *Amoretti*, Richard Barnfield's *Cynthia*, Barnes' *Century of Spiritual Sonnets*, the anonymous *Alcilia*: in 1596 Bartholomew Griffin's *Fidessa* and William Smith's *Chloris*: in 1597 Henry Lok's *Century of Christian Passions*, Robert Tofte's *Laura*, Nicholas Breton's *Arbour of Amorous Devices*: in 1598 Tofte's *Alba*. Thereafter the publication of sonnets entirely ceased for several years.

It is likeliest therefore that Shakespeare's Sonnets were written during this vogue, that is, between 1592 and 1598. In style they are akin rather to *Venus and Adonis* and some of the earlier plays, and detailed comparisons which have been made show that the greatest number of parallels of phrase and idea are to be found in *Love's Labour's Lost*, *The Two Gentlemen of Verona*, *Romeo and Juliet*, *Venus and Adonis*, *Lucrece*, *Richard II*, and *Richard III*, all of which were written by 1595.

There may be some hint of the scandal referred to in Sonnet 36 in *Willobie his Avisa*, which is a collection of poems written dialogue-wise in eighty-four cantos. The book first appeared in 1594; it was reprinted in 1596, and was regarded as in some way personal and scandalous, for in June 1599 a third edition was called in, together with other seditious and scandalous books of satire. It was a popular book, reprinted in 1605, 1609 and 1635.

Willobie his Avisa tells the story of a certain woman of humble birth, whom the author calls Avisa. She was the wife of an innkeeper who attracted many admirers, including noblemen, all of whom she rejected. Amongst the suitors is a certain young man, 'H. W.', who takes Avisa's refusal more unkindly than the rest and 'being suddenly infected with the contagion of a fantastical fit, at the first sight of A, pineth a while in secret grief, at length not able any longer to endure the burning heat of so fervent a humour, bewrayeth the secrecy of his disease unto his familiar friend W. S. who not long before had tried the courtesy of the like passion, and was now newly recovered of the like infection; yet finding his friend let blood in the same vein, he took pleasure for a time to see him bleed, and instead of stopping the issue, he enlargeth the wound, with the sharp razor of a willing conceit, persuading him that he thought it a matter very easy to be compassed, and no doubt with pain, diligence and some cost in time to be obtained. Thus this miserable comforter comforting his friend with an impossibility, either for that he now would secretly laugh at his friend's folly, that had given occasion not long before unto others to laugh at his own, or because he would see whether another could play his part better than himself, and in viewing afar off the course of this loving comedy, he determined to see whether it would sort to a happier end for this new actor, than it did for the old player. But at length this comedy was like to have grown to a tragedy, by the weak and feeble estate that H. W. was brought unto, by a desperate view of an impossibility of obtaining his purpose, till Time and Necessity, being his best physicians brought him a plaster, if not to heal, yet in part to ease his malady. In all which discourse is lively represented the unruly rage of unbridled fancy, having the reins to rove at liberty, with the divers and sundry changes of affections and temptations, which Will, set loose from Reason, can devise.'

Willobie his Avisa itself is as great a puzzle as the Sonnets, but it seems reasonably likely that by W. S. the 'old player' Shakespeare himself is implied; and if so, that 'H. W.' may be the friend of the Sonnets.*

* I have tried to unravel the story in my edition of *Willobie his Avisa*.

V

At the present time the case for identifying the fair youth with Henry Wriothesley, Earl of Southampton, seems to be stronger than the others. Certainly, his initials are H. W., and not W. H. and he was not a 'Mr'. On the other hand the dedication of the Sonnets is equivocal, for only the author, and not the recipient, can accurately be called the 'begetter' of a sonnet.

If this identification of the fair youth is correct then the known facts (such as are known) of the life of Shakespeare and of Southampton tally with the story of the Sonnets. Southampton was born on 6th October 1573, and succeeded to the title at the age of seven. He was therefore a ward until he came of age, Lord Burghley being his guardian. Shakespeare dedicated *Venus and Adonis,* which was entered for publication on the 18th April 1593, to Southampton in these words:

'To the Right Honourable Henry Wriothesley, Earl of Southampton, and Baron of Titchfield.

'Right Honourable, I know not how I shall offend in dedicating my unpolished lines to your Lordship, nor how the world will censure me for choosing so strong a prop to support so weak a burthen, only if your Honour seem but pleased, I account myself highly praised, and vow to take advantage of all idle hours, till I have honoured you with some graver labour. But if the first heir of my invention prove deformed, I shall be sorry it had so noble a godfather: and never after ear so barren a land, for fear it yield me still so bad a harvest. I leave it to your honourable survey, and your Honour to your heart's content which I wish may always answer your own wish, and the world's hopeful expectation.

> 'Your Honour's in all duty,
> 'WILLIAM SHAKESPEARE.'

In 1594 he dedicated *Lucrece* (entered 9th May) to him in much warmer terms:

> 'To the Right Honourable, Henry Wriothesley, Earl of Southampton, and Baron of Titchfield.
> 'The love I dedicate to your Lordship is without end: whereof this Pamphlet without beginning is but a superfluous moiety. The warrant I have of your honourable disposition, not the worth of my untutored lines makes it assured of acceptance. What I have done is yours, what I have to do is yours, being part in all I have, devoted yours. Were my worth greater, my duty would show greater, meantime, as it is, it is bound to your Lordship; to whom I wish long life still lengthened with all happiness.
> 'Your Lordship's in all duty,
> 'WILLIAM SHAKESPEARE.'

Southampton as a young man was conspicuously handsome, and, to the embarrassment of his relatives, he refused to marry, although Lord Burghley himself proposed his own grand-daughter, Lady Elizabeth Vere. In 1594 Southampton was obliged to pay £5,000 for Lady Elizabeth's blighted affections. In 1595 he fell in love with Mistress Elizabeth Vernon, one of Queen Elizabeth's Maids of Honour, whom he secretly married in 1598. Southampton was a great admirer and personal friend of the Earl of Essex. He was with Essex in the Islands Voyage of 1597, and in Ireland in 1599. In 1601 he took part in the Essex rebellion. He was tried with Essex and condemned to death, but his life was spared and he remained a prisoner in the Tower until the death of Queen Elizabeth. The story of the Sonnets thus fits in with the lives of Southampton and of Shakespeare.

Another nobleman who has been proposed is William Herbert, Earl of Pembroke. He was born in 1580. To him and to his brother, Philip Herbert, Earl of Montgomery, Heminge and Condell dedicated the First Folio of Shakespeare's plays in 1623, 'since your Lordships have been pleased to think these trifles somewhat heretofore, and have prosecuted both them and their Author living with so much favour'. His initials are 'W. H.', though it is doubtful whether anyone even in a cryptic dedication would refer to him as 'Mr' in 1609. In 1595 there was a proposal to betroth him to the daughter of Sir George Carey, son of the patron of the Lord Chamberlain's Company. Nothing further is known of any connexion between him and Shakespeare.

Various other candidates have been put forward. Some, taking line 7 of Sonnet 20 in its original spelling,

'A man in hew all *Hews* in his controwling',

believe that it puns on the name Hughes, and that the original youth was named William Hughes, a boy actor who took women's parts. The records of Elizabethan acting companies are fairly complete, but there is no trace of any actor of this name.

It is also possible that all the theories are mistaken, and that the beautiful youth was some quite different person.

VI

Of *A Lover's Complaint* nothing is known. It appeared first as an appendix to the Sonnets without comment or introduction. Some critics do not believe that Shakespeare wrote it. Such poems often describe real events but the complaint of a deserted mistress is too common for the characters to be identified. It is worth noting that there are several similar poems written in the 1590's, such as Anthony Chutes' *Beauty Dishonoured,* the lament of Mistress Jane Shore, mistress of Edward IV, and Samuel Daniel's *Rosamond's Complaint.*

VII

The text of the 1609 Quarto of the *Sonnets* and *A Lover's Complaint* is fairly good, with a few misprints or errors. The punctuation is inconsistent. At one time it is subtle and striking, at another obviously wrong.

Another version of the Sonnets appeared in 1640 as 'Poems: Written by Wil. Shakespeare, Gent. Printed at London by Tho. Cotes, and are to be sold by John Benson, dwelling in St. Dunstan's Churchyard'. In this edition various additional poems were included. The Sonnets were reprinted in a new order, and alterations made so that the Sonnets read as if addressed to a woman. Apart from this version they were not again reprinted during the seventeenth century, and for several generations they were forgotten until interest in them was revived at the end of the eighteenth century.

The present text follows the quarto of 1609 closely. Spelling is modernized but the punctuation and general arrangement has been kept except where either seemed indefensible or confusing.

*

The Sonnets

TO. THE. ONLY. BEGETTER. OF.
THESE. INSUING. SONNETS.
MR. W. H. ALL. HAPPINESS.
AND. THAT. ETERNITY.
PROMISED.
BY.
OUR. EVER-LIVING. POET.
WISHETH.
THE. WELL-WISHING.
ADVENTURER. IN.
SETTING.
FORTH.
T.T.

1

From fairest creatures we desire increase,
That thereby beauty's rose might never die,
But as the riper should by time decease,
His tender heir might bear his memory:
But thou contracted to thine own bright eyes,
Feed'st thy light's flame with self substantial fuel,
Making a famine where abundance lies,
Thyself thy foe, to thy sweet self too cruel:
Thou that art now the world's fresh ornament,
And only herald to the gaudy spring,
Within thine own bud buriest thy content,
And tender churl mak'st waste in niggarding:
    Pity the world, or else this glutton be,
    To eat the world's due, by the grave and thee.

2

When forty winters shall besiege thy brow,
And dig deep trenches in thy beauty's field,
Thy youth's proud livery so gaz'd on now,
Will be a totter'd weed of small worth held:
Then being ask'd, where all thy beauty lies,
Where all the treasure of thy lusty days;
To say within thine own deep sunken eyes,
Were an all-eating shame, and thriftless praise.
How much more praise deserv'd thy beauty's use,
If thou could'st answer this fair child of mine
Shall sum my count, and make my old excuse
Proving his beauty by succession thine.
    This were to be new made when thou art old,
    And see thy blood warm when thou feel'st it cold.

3

Look in thy glass and tell the face thou viewest,
Now is the time that face should form another,
Whose fresh repair if now thou not renewest,
Thou dost beguile the world, unbless some mother.
For where is she so fair whose unear'd womb
Disdains the tillage of thy husbandry?
Or who is he so fond will be the tomb,
Of his self-love to stop posterity?
Thou art thy mother's glass and she in thee
Calls back the lovely April of her prime,
So thou through windows of thine age shalt see,
Despite of wrinkles this thy golden time.
   But if thou live remember'd not to be,
   Die single and thine Image dies with thee.

4

Unthrifty loveliness why dost thou spend,
Upon thyself thy beauty's legacy?
Nature's bequest gives nothing but doth lend,
And being frank she lends to those are free:
Then beauteous niggard why dost thou abuse,
The bounteous largess given thee to give?
Profitless usurer why dost thou use
So great a sum of sums yet canst not live?
For having traffic with thyself alone,
Thou of thyself thy sweet self dost deceive,
Then how when nature calls thee to be gone,
What acceptable audit canst thou leave?
   Thy unus'd beauty must be tomb'd with thee,
   Which used lives th' executor to be.

5

Those hours that with gentle work did frame,
The lovely gaze where every eye doth dwell
Will play the tyrants to the very same,
And that unfair which fairly doth excel:
For never resting time leads summer on,
To hideous winter and confounds him there,
Sap check'd with frost and lusty leaves quite gone,
Beauty o'ersnow'd and bareness everywhere:
Then were not summer's distillation left
A liquid prisoner pent in walls of glass,
Beauty's effect with beauty were bereft,
Nor it nor no remembrance what it was.
   But flowers distill'd though they with winter meet,
   Leese but their show, their substance still lives sweet.

6

Then let not winter's ragged hand deface,
In thee thy summer ere thou be distill'd:
Make sweet some vial; treasure thou some place,
With beauty's treasure ere it be self kill'd:
That use is not forbidden usury,
Which happies those that pay the willing loan;
That's for thyself to breed another thee,
Or ten times happier be it ten for one,
Ten times thyself were happier than thou art,
If ten of thine ten times refigur'd thee,
Then what could death do if thou shouldst depart,
Leaving thee living in posterity?
   Be not self-will'd for thou art much too fair,
   To be death's conquest and make worms thine heir.

7

Lo in the Orient when the gracious light,
Lifts up his burning head, each under eye
Doth homage to his new appearing sight,
Serving with looks his sacred majesty,
And having climb'd the steep up heavenly hill,
Resembling strong youth in his middle age,
Yet mortal looks adore his beauty still,
Attending on his golden pilgrimage:
But when from high-most pitch with weary car,
Like feeble age he reeleth from the day,
The eyes ('fore duteous) now converted are
From his low tract and look another way:
    So thou, thyself out-going in thy noon,
    Unlook'd on diest unless thou get a son.

8

Music to hear, why hear'st thou music sadly?
Sweets with sweets war not, joy delights in joy:
Why lov'st thou that which thou receiv'st not gladly,
Or else receiv'st with pleasure thine annoy?
If the true concord of well tuned sounds,
By unions married do offend thine ear,
They do but sweetly chide thee, who confounds
In singleness the parts that thou should'st bear:
Mark how one string sweet husband to another,
Strikes each in each by mutual ordering;
Resembling sire, and child, and happy mother,
Who all in one, one pleasing note do sing:
    Whose speechless song being many, seeming one,
    Sings this to thee thou single wilt prove none.

9

Is it for fear to wet a widow's eye,
That thou consum'st thyself in single life?
Ah; if thou issueless shalt hap to die,
The world will wail thee like a makeless wife,
The world will be thy widow and still weep,
That thou no form of thee hast left behind,
When every private widow well may keep,
By children's eyes, her husband's shape in mind:
Look what an unthrift in the world doth spend
Shifts but his place, for still the world enjoys it:
But beauty's waste hath in the world an end,
And kept unus'd the user so destroys it:
No love toward others in that bosom sits
That on himself such murd'rous shame commits.

10

For shame deny that thou bear'st love to any
Who for thyself art so unprovident:
Grant if thou wilt, thou art belov'd of many,
But that thou none lov'st is most evident:
For thou art so possess'd with murd'rous hate,
That 'gainst thyself thou stick'st not to conspire,
Seeking that beauteous roof to ruinate
Which to repair should be thy chief desire:
O change thy thought, that I may change my mind,
Shall hate be fairer lodg'd than gentle love?
Be as thy presence is gracious and kind,
Or to thyself at least kind-hearted prove,
Make thee another self for love of me,
That beauty still may live in thine or thee.

11

As fast as thou shalt wane so fast thou grow'st,
In one of thine, from that which thou departest,
And that fresh blood which youngly thou bestow'st,
Thou mayst call thine, when thou from youth convertest,
Herein lives wisdom, beauty, and increase,
Without this folly, age, and cold decay,
If all were minded so, the times should cease,
And threescore year would make the world away:
Let those whom nature hath not made for store,
Harsh, featureless, and rude, barrenly perish:
Look whom she best endow'd, she gave the more;
Which bounteous gift thou shouldst in bounty cherish,
  She carv'd thee for her seal, and meant thereby,
  Thou shouldst print more, not let that copy die.

12

When I do count the clock that tells the time,
And see the brave day sunk in hideous night,
When I behold the violet past prime,
And sable curls all silver'd o'er with white:
When lofty trees I see barren of leaves,
Which erst from heat did canopy the herd
And Summer's green all girded up in sheaves
Borne on the bier with white and bristly beard:
Then of thy beauty do I question make
That thou among the wastes of time must go,
Since sweets and beauties do themselves forsake,
And die as fast as they see others grow,
  And nothing 'gainst Time's scythe can make defence
  Saved breed to brave him, when he takes thee hence.

13

O that you were yourself, but love you are
No longer yours, than you yourself here live,
Against this coming end you should prepare,
And your sweet semblance to some other give.
So should that beauty which you hold in lease
Find no determination, then you were
Yourself again after yourself's decease,
When your sweet issue your sweet form should bear.
Who lets so fair a house fall to decay,
Which husbandry in honour might uphold,
Against the stormy gusts of winter's day
And barren rage of death's eternal cold?
   O none but unthrifts, dear my love you know,
   You had a Father, let your Son say so.

14

Not from the stars do I my judgment pluck,
And yet methinks I have Astronomy,
But not to tell of good, or evil luck,
Of plagues, of dearths, or season's quality;
Nor can I fortune to brief minutes tell,
Pointing to each his thunder, rain, and wind,
Or say with Princes if it shall go well
By oft predict that I in heaven find.
But from thine eyes my knowledge I derive,
And constant stars in them I read such art
As truth and beauty shall together thrive
If from thyself, to store thou wouldst convert:
   Or else of thee this I prognosticate,
   Thy end is Truth's and Beauty's doom and date.

15

When I consider everything that grows
Holds in perfection but a little moment.
That this huge stage presenteth nought but shows
Whereon the Stars in secret influence comment.
When I perceive that men as plants increase,
Cheered and check'd even by the selfsame sky:
Vaunt in their youthful sap, at height decrease,
And wear their brave state out of memory.
Then the conceit of this inconstant stay,
Sets you most rich in youth before my sight,
Where wasteful time debateth with decay
To change your day of youth to sullied night,
    And all in war with Time for love of you
    As he takes from you, I engraft you new.

16

But wherefore do not you a mightier way
Make war upon this bloody tyrant Time?
And fortify yourself in your decay
With means more blessed than my barren rhyme?
Now stand you on the top of happy hours,
And many maiden gardens yet unset,
With virtuous wish would bear your living flowers,
Much liker than your painted counterfeit:
So should the lines of life that life repair
Which this (Time's pencil or my pupil pen)
Neither in inward worth nor outward fair
Can make you live yourself in eyes of men:
    To give away yourself, keeps yourself still,
    And you must live drawn by your own sweet skill.

17

Who will believe my verse in time to come
If it were fill'd with your most high deserts?
Though yet heaven knows it is but as a tomb
Which hides your life, and shows not half your parts:
If I could write the beauty of your eyes,
And in fresh numbers number all your graces,
The age to come would say this Poet lies,
Such heavenly touches ne'er touch'd earthly faces.
So should my papers (yellowed with their age)
Be scorn'd, like old men of less truth than tongue,
And your true rights be term'd a Poet's rage,
And stretched metre of an antique song.
    But were some child of yours alive that time,
    You should live twice, in it and in my rhyme.

18

Shall I compare thee to a Summer's day?
Thou art more lovely and more temperate:
Rough winds do shake the darling buds of May,
And Summer's lease hath all too short a date:
Sometime too hot the eye of heaven shines,
And often is his gold complexion dimm'd,
And every fair from fair sometime declines,
By chance, or nature's changing course untrimm'd:
But thy eternal Summer shall not fade,
Nor lose possession of that fair thou ow'st,
Nor shall Death brag thou wander'st in his shade,
When in eternal lines to time thou grow'st:
    So long as men can breathe or eyes can see,
    So long lives this, and this gives life to thee.

B

19

Devouring Time blunt thou the Lion's paws,
And make the earth devour her own sweet brood,
Pluck the keen teeth from the fierce Tiger's jaws,
And burn the long-liv'd Phoenix in her blood,
Make glad and sorry seasons as thou fleet'st,
And do whate'er thou wilt, swift-footed Time,
To the wide world and all her fading sweets :
But I forbid thee one most heinous crime,
O carve not with thy hours my love's fair brow,
Nor draw no lines there with thine antique pen,
Him in thy course untainted do allow,
For beauty's pattern to succeeding men.
*   Yet do thy worst old Time, despite thy wrong,*
*   My love shall in my verse ever live young.*

20

A woman's face with Nature's own hand painted,
Hast thou the Master Mistress of my passion,
A woman's gentle heart but not acquainted
With shifting change as is false women's fashion,
An eye more bright than theirs, less false in rolling,
Gilding the object whereupon it gazeth,
A man in hue all hues in his controlling,
Which steals men's eyes and women's souls amazeth.
And for a woman wert thou first created,
Till Nature as she wrought thee fell a-doting,
And by addition me of thee defeated,
By adding one thing to my purpose nothing.
*   But since she prick'd thee out for women's pleasure,*
*   Mine be thy love and thy love's use their treasure.*

21

So is it not with me as with that Muse,
Stirr'd by a painted beauty to his verse,
Who heaven itself for ornament doth use,
And every fair with his fair doth rehearse,
Making a couplement of proud compare
With Sun and Moon, with earth and sea's rich gems:
With April's first-born flowers and all things rare,
That heaven's air in this huge rondure hems,
O let me true in love but truly write,
And then believe me, my love is as fair,
As any mother's child, though not so bright
As those gold candles fix'd in heaven's air:
    Let them say more that like of hearsay well,
    I will not praise that purpose not to sell.

22

My glass shall not persuade me I am old,
So long as youth and thou are of one date,
But when in thee time's furrows I behold,
Then look I death my days should expiate.
For all that beauty that doth cover thee,
Is but the seemly raiment of my heart,
Which in thy breast doth live, as thine in me,
How can I then be elder than thou art?
O therefore love be of thyself so wary,
As I not for myself, but for thee will,
Bearing thy heart which I will keep so chary
As tender nurse her babe from faring ill,
    Presume not on thy heart when mine is slain,
    Thou gav'st me thine not to give back again.

23

As an unperfect actor on the stage,
Who with his fear is put besides his part,
Or some fierce thing replete with too much rage,
Whose strength's abundance weakens his own heart;
So I for fear of trust, forget to say,
The perfect ceremony of love's rite,
And in mine own love's strength seem to decay,
O'ercharg'd with burthen of mine own love's might:
O let my books be then the eloquence,
And dumb presagers of my speaking breast,
Who plead for love, and look for recompense,
More than that tongue that more hath more express'd.
    O learn to read what silent love hath writ,
    To hear with eyes belongs to love's fine wit.

24

Mine eye hath play'd the painter and hath steel'd
Thy beauty's form in table of my heart,
My body is the frame wherein 't is held,
And perspective it is best Painter's art.
For through the Painter must you see his skill,
To find where your true Image pictur'd lies,
Which in my bosom's shop is hanging still,
That hath his windows glazed with thine eyes:
Now see what good turns eyes for eyes have done,
Mine eyes have drawn thy shape, and thine for me
Are windows to my breast, where-through the Sun
Delights to peep, to gaze therein on thee.
    Yet eyes this cunning want to grace their art,
    They draw but what they see, know not the heart.

25

Let those who are in favour with their stars,
Of public honour and proud titles boast,
Whilst I whom fortune of such triumph bars
Unlook'd for joy in that I honour most;
Great Princes' favourites their fair leaves spread,
But as the marigold at the sun's eye,
And in themselves their pride lies buried,
For at a frown they in their glory die.
The painful warrior famoused for worth,
After a thousand victories once foil'd,
Is from the book of honour razed forth,
And all the rest forgot for which he toil'd:
   Then happy I that love and am beloved
   Where I may not remove, nor be removed.

26

Lord of my love, to whom in vassalage
Thy merit hath my duty strongly knit;
To thee I send this written ambassage
To witness duty, not to show my wit.
Duty so great, which wit so poor as mine
May make seem bare, in wanting words to show it;
But that I hope some good conceit of thine
In thy soul's thought (all naked) will bestow it:
Till whatsoever star that guides my moving,
Points on me graciously with fair aspect,
And puts apparel on my tottered loving,
To show me worthy of thy sweet respect:
   Then may I dare to boast how I do love thee,
   Till then, not show my head where thou mayst prove me.

27

Weary with toil, I haste me to my bed,
The dear repose for limbs with travel tired,
But then begins a journey in my head
To work my mind, when body's work's expired.
For then my thoughts (from far where I abide)
Intend a zealous pilgrimage to thee,
And keep my drooping eyelids open wide,
Looking on darkness which the blind do see.
Save that my soul's imaginary sight
Presents thy shadow to my sightless view,
Which like a jewel (hung in ghastly night)
Makes black night beauteous, and her old face new.
   Lo thus by day my limbs, by night my mind,
   For thee, and for myself, no quiet find.

28

How can I then return in happy plight
That am debarr'd the benefit of rest?
When day's oppression is not eas'd by night,
But day by night and night by day oppress'd.
And each (though enemies to either's reign)
Do in consent shake hands to torture me,
The one by toil, the other to complain
How far I toil, still farther off from thee.
I tell the day to please him thou art bright,
And dost him grace when clouds do blot the heaven:
So flatter I the swart-complexion'd night,
When sparkling stars twire not thou gild'st th' even.
   But day doth daily draw my sorrows longer,
   And night doth nightly make grief's length seem stronger.

29

When in disgrace with Fortune and men's eyes,
I all alone beweep my outcast state,
And trouble deaf heaven with my bootless cries,
And look upon myself and curse my fate,
Wishing me like to one more rich in hope,
Featur'd like him, like him with friends possess'd,
Desiring this man's art, and that man's scope,
With what I most enjoy contented least,
Yet in these thoughts myself almost despising,
Haply I think on thee, and then my state
(Like to the lark at break of day arising),
From sullen earth sings hymns at Heaven's gate,
 For thy sweet love remember'd such wealth brings,
 That then I scorn to change my state with Kings.

30

When to the sessions of sweet silent thought,
I summon up remembrance of things past,
I sigh the lack of many a thing I sought,
And with old woes new wail my dear times' waste:
Then can I drown an eye (unus'd to flow)
For precious friends hid in death's dateless night,
And weep afresh love's long-since cancell'd woe,
And moan th' expense of many a vanish'd sight.
Then can I grieve at grievances foregone,
And heavily from woe to woe tell o'er
The sad account of fore-bemoaned moan,
Which I new pay, as if not paid before.
 But if the while I think on thee (dear friend)
 All losses are restor'd, and sorrows end.

31

Thy bosom is endeared with all hearts,
Which I by lacking have supposed dead,
And there reigns Love and all Love's loving parts,
And all those friends which I thought buried.
How many a holy and obsequious tear
Hath dear religious love stolen from mine eye,
As interest of the dead, which now appear,
But things remov'd that hidden in thee lie.
Thou art the grave where buried love doth live,
Hung with the trophies of my lovers gone,
Who all their parts of me to thee did give,
That due of many, now is thine alone.
    Their images I lov'd, I view in thee,
    And thou (all they) hast all the all of me.

32

If thou survive my well-contented day,
When that churl Death my bones with dust shall cover
And shalt by fortune once more re-survey
These poor rude lines of thy deceased lover:
Compare them with the bett'ring of the time,
And though they be outstripp'd by every pen,
Reserve them for my love, not for their rhyme,
Exceeded by the height of happier men.
Oh then vouchsafe me but this loving thought,
Had my friend's Muse grown with this growing age,
A dearer birth than this his love had brought
To march in ranks of better equipage:
    But since he died and Poets better prove,
    Theirs for their style I'll read, his for his love.

33

Full many a glorious morning have I seen,
Flatter the mountain-tops with sovereign eye,
Kissing with golden face the meadows green,
Gilding pale streams with heavenly alchymy:
Anon permit the basest clouds to ride,
With ugly rack on his celestial face,
And from the forlorn world his visage hide
Stealing unseen to west with this disgrace:
Even so my Sun one early morn did shine,
With all triumphant splendour on my brow,
But out alack, he was but one hour mine,
The region cloud hath mask'd him from me now.
   Yet him for this, my love no whit disdaineth,
   Suns of the world may stain, when heaven's sun staineth.

34

Why didst thou promise such a beauteous day,
And make me travel forth without my cloak,
To let base clouds o'ertake me in my way,
Hiding thy brav'ry in their rotten smoke.
'Tis not enough that through the cloud thou break,
To dry the rain on my storm-beaten face,
For no man well of such a salve can speak,
That heals the wound, and cures not the disgrace:
Nor can thy shame give physic to my grief,
Though thou repent, yet I have still the loss,
Th' offender's sorrow lends but weak relief
To him that bears the strong offence's cross.
   Ah but those tears are pearl which thy love sheds,
   And they are rich, and ransom all ill deeds.

35

No more be griev'd at that which thou hast done,
Roses have thorns, and silver fountains mud,
Clouds and eclipses stain both Moon and Sun,
And loathsome canker lives in sweetest bud.
All men make faults, and even I in this,
Authorizing thy trespass with compare,
Myself corrupting salving thy amiss,
Excusing thy sins more than thy sins are:
For to thy sensual fault I bring in sense,
Thy adverse party is thy advocate,
And 'gainst myself a lawful plea commence,
Such civil war is in my love and hate,
 That I an accessory needs must be,
 To that sweet thief which sourly robs from me.

36

Let me confess that we two must be twain,
Although our undivided loves are one:
So shall those blots that do with me remain,
Without thy help, by me be borne alone.
In our two loves there is but one respect,
Though in our lives a separable spite,
Which though it alter not love's sole effect,
Yet doth it steal sweet hours from love's delight.
I may not evermore acknowledge thee,
Lest my bewailed guilt should do thee shame,
Nor thou with public kindness honour me,
Unless thou take that honour from thy name:
 But do not so, I love thee in such sort,
 As thou being mine, mine is thy good report.

37

As a decrepit father takes delight,
To see his active child do deeds of youth,
So I, made lame by Fortune's dearest spite
Take all my comfort of thy worth and truth.
For whether beauty, birth, or wealth, or wit,
Or any of these all, or all, or more
Entitled in thy parts, do crowned sit,
I make my love engrafted to this store:
So then I am not lame, poor, nor despis'd,
Whilst that this shadow doth such substance give,
That I in thy abundance am suffic'd,
And by a part of all thy glory live:
  Look what is best, that best I wish in thee,
  This wish I have, then ten times happy me.

38

How can my Muse want subject to invent
While thou dost breathe that pour'st into my verse,
Thine own sweet argument, too excellent,
For every vulgar paper to rehearse:
Oh give thyself the thanks if aught in me,
Worthy perusal stand against thy sight,
For who's so dumb that cannot write to thee,
When thou thyself dost give invention light?
Be thou the tenth Muse, ten times more in worth
Than those old nine which rhymers invocate,
And he that calls on thee, let him bring forth
Eternal numbers to outlive long date.
  If my slight Muse do please these curious days,
  The pain be mine, but thine shall be the praise.

39

Oh how thy worth with manners may I sing,
When thou art all the better part of me?
What can mine own praise to mine own self bring?
And what is 't but mine own when I praise thee?
Even for this, let us divided live,
And our dear love lose name of single one,
That by this separation I may give
That due to thee which thou deserv'st alone:
Oh absence what a torment wouldst thou prove,
Were it not thy sour leisure gave sweet leave,
To entertain the time with thoughts of love,
Which time and thoughts so sweetly doth deceive,
   And that thou teachest how to make one twain,
   By praising him here who doth hence remain.

40

Take all my loves, my love, yea take them all,
What hast thou then more than thou hadst before?
No love, my love, that thou mayst true love call,
All mine was thine, before thou hadst this more:
Then if for my love, thou my love receivest,
I cannot blame thee, for my love thou usest,
But yet be blam'd, if thou thyself deceivest
By wilful taste of what thyself refusest.
I do forgive thy robb'ry gentle thief
Although thou steal thee all my poverty:
And yet love knows it is a greater grief
To bear love's wrong, than hate's known injury.
   Lascivious grace in whom all ill well shows,
   Kill me with spites yet we must not be foes.

41

Those pretty wrongs that liberty commits,
When I am sometime absent from thy heart,
Thy beauty, and thy years full well befits,
For still temptation follows where thou art.
Gentle thou art, and therefore to be won,
Beauteous thou art, therefore to be assailed.
And when a woman woos, what woman's son
Will sourly leave her till he have prevailed.
Aye me, but yet thou mightst my seat forbear,
And chide thy beauty, and thy straying youth,
Who lead thee in their riot even there
Where thou art forc'd to break a two-fold truth:
    Hers by thy beauty tempting her to thee,
    Thine by thy beauty being false to me.

42

That thou hast her it is not all my grief,
And yet it may be said I lov'd her dearly,
That she hath thee is of my wailing chief,
A loss in love that touches me more nearly.
Loving offenders thus I will excuse ye,
Thou dost love her, because thou know'st I love her,
And for my sake even so doth she abuse me,
Suff'ring my friend for my sake to approve her:
If I lose thee, my loss is my love's gain,
And losing her, my friend hath found that loss,
Both find each other, and I lose both twain,
And both for my sake lay on me this cross:
    But here's the joy, my friend and I are one,
    Sweet flattery, then she loves but me alone.

43

When most I wink then do mine eyes best see,
For all the day they view things unrespected,
But when I sleep, in dreams they look on thee,
And darkly bright, are bright in dark directed.
Then thou whose shadow shadows doth make bright,
How would thy shadow's form, form happy show,
To the clear day with thy much clearer light,
When to unseeing eyes thy shade shines so?
How would (I say) mine eyes be blessed made,
By looking on thee in the living day?
When in dead night thy fair imperfect shade
Through heavy sleep on sightless eyes doth stay?
    All days are nights to see till I see thee,
    And nights bright days when dreams do show thee me.

44

If the dull substance of my flesh were thought,
Injurious distance should not stop my way,
For then despite of space I would be brought,
From limits far remote, where thou dost stay.
No matter then although my foot did stand
Upon the farthest earth remov'd from thee,
For nimble thought can jump both sea and land,
As soon as think the place where he would be.
But ah, thought kills me that I am not thought
To leap large lengths of miles when thou art gone,
But that so much of earth and water wrought,
I must attend time's leisure with my moan.
    Receiving nought by elements so slow,
    But heavy tears, badges of either's woe.

45

The other two, slight air, and purging fire,
Are both with thee, wherever I abide,
The first my thought, the other my desire,
These present absent with swift motion slide.
For when these quicker elements are gone
In tender embassy of love to thee,
My life being made of four, with two alone,
Sinks down to death, oppress'd with melancholy.
Until life's composition be recured,
By those swift messengers return'd from thee,
Who even but now come back again assured,
Of thy fair health, recounting it to me.
    This told, I joy, but then no longer glad,
    I send them back again and straight grow sad.

46

Mine eye and heart are at a mortal war,
How to divide the conquest of thy sight,
Mine eye, my heart thy picture's sight would bar,
My heart, mine eye the freedom of that right,
My heart doth plead that thou in him dost lie
(A closet never pierc'd with crystal eyes),
But the defendant doth that plea deny,
And says in him thy fair appearance lies.
To 'cide this title is impannelled
A quest of thoughts, all tenants to the heart,
And by their verdict is determined
The clear eye's moiety, and the dear heart's part.
    As thus, mine eye's due is thine outward part,
    And my heart's right, thine inward love of heart.

47

Betwixt mine eye and heart a league is took,
And each doth good turns now unto the other,
When that mine eye is famish'd for a look,
Or heart in love with sighs himself doth smother;
With my love's picture then my eye doth feast,
And to the painted banquet bids my heart:
Another time mine eye is my heart's guest,
And in his thoughts of love doth share a part.
So either by thy picture or my love,
Thyself away, art present still with me,
For thou not farther than my thoughts canst move,
And I am still with them, and they with thee.
   Or if they sleep, thy picture in my sight
   Awakes my heart, to heart's and eye's delight.

48

How careful was I when I took my way,
Each trifle under truest bars to thrust,
That to my use it might unused stay
From hands of falsehood, in sure wards of trust?
But thou, to whom my jewels trifles are,
Most worthy comfort, now my greatest grief,
Thou best of dearest, and mine only care,
Art left the prey of every vulgar thief.
Thee have I not lock'd up in any chest,
Save where thou art not, though I feel thou art,
Within the gentle closure of my breast,
From whence at pleasure thou mayst come and part,
   And even thence thou wilt be stolen I fear,
   For truth proves thievish for a prize so dear.

49

Against that time (if ever that time come)
When I shall see thee frown on my defects,
Whenas thy love hath cast his utmost sum,
Call'd to that audit by advis'd respects,
Against that time when thou shalt strangely pass,
And scarcely greet me with that sun thine eye,
When love converted from the thing it was
Shall reasons find of settled gravity.
Against that time do I ensconce me here
Within the knowledge of mine own desart,
And this my hand, against myself uprear,
To guard the lawful reasons on thy part,
     To leave poor me, thou hast the strength of laws,
     Since why to love, I can allege no cause.

50

How heavy do I journey on the way,
When what I seek (my weary travel's end)
Doth teach that ease and that repose to say
Thus far the miles are measur'd from thy friend.
The beast that bears me, tired with my woe,
Plods dully on, to bear that weight in me,
As if by some instinct the wretch did know
His rider lov'd not speed being made from thee:
The bloody spur cannot provoke him on,
That sometimes anger thrusts into his hide,
Which heavily he answers with a groan,
More sharp to me than spurring to his side,
     For that same groan doth put this in my mind,
     My grief lies onward and my joy behind.

51

Thus can my love excuse the slow offence,
Of my dull bearer, when from thee I speed,
From where thou art, why should I haste me thence,
Till I return of posting is no need.
O what excuse will my poor beast then find,
When swift extremity can seem but slow,
Then should I spur though mounted on the wind,
In winged speed no motion shall I know.
Then can no horse with my desire keep pace,
Therefore desire (of perfect'st love being made)
Shall neigh, no dull flesh in his fiery race,
But love, for love, thus shall excuse my jade,
　　Since from thee going he went wilful slow,
　　Towards thee I'll run, and give him leave to go.

52

So am I as the rich whose blessed key,
Can bring him to his sweet up-locked treasure,
The which he will not ev'ry hour survey,
For blunting the fine point of seldom pleasure.
Therefore are feasts so solemn and so rare,
Since seldom coming in the long year set,
Like stones of worth they thinly placed are,
Or captain jewels in the carcanet.
So is the time that keeps you as my chest,
Or as the wardrobe which the robe doth hide,
To make some special instant special blest,
By new unfolding his imprison'd pride.
　　Blessed are you whose worthiness gives scope,
　　Being had to triumph, being lack'd to hope.

53

What is your substance, whereof are you made,
That millions of strange shadows on you tend?
Since every one hath, every one, one shade,
And you but one, can every shadow lend:
Describe Adonis and the counterfeit,
Is poorly imitated after you,
On Helen's cheek all art of beauty set,
And you in Grecian tires are painted new:
Speak of the spring, and foizon of the year,
The one doth shadow of your beauty show,
The other as your bounty doth appear,
And you in every blessed shape we know.
 In all external grace you have some part,
 But you like none, none you for constant heart.

54

Oh how much more doth beauty beauteous seem,
By that sweet ornament which truth doth give,
The rose looks fair, but fairer we it deem
For that sweet odour, which doth in it live:
The canker-blooms have full as deep a dye,
As the perfumed tincture of the roses,
Hang on such thorns, and play as wantonly,
When summer's breath their masked buds discloses:
But for their virtue only is their show,
They live unwoo'd, and unrespected fade,
Die to themselves. Sweet roses do not so, ·
Of their sweet deaths, are sweetest odours made:
 And so of you, beauteous and lovely youth,
 When that shall vade, my verse distils your truth.

55

Not marble, nor the gilded monuments
Of Princes shall outlive this powerful rhyme,
But you shall shine more bright in these contents
Than unswept stone, besmear'd with sluttish time.
When wasteful war shall statues overturn,
And broils root out the work of masonry,
Nor Mars his sword, nor war's quick fire shall burn
The living record of your memory.
'Gainst death, and all-oblivious enmity
Shall you pace forth, your praise shall still find room,
Even in the eyes of all posterity
That wear this world out to the ending doom.
 So till the judgment that yourself arise,
  You live in this, and dwell in lovers' eyes.

56

Sweet love renew thy force, be it not said
Thy edge should blunter be than appetite,
Which but today by feeding is allay'd,
Tomorrow sharpened in his former might.
So love be thou, although today thou fill
Thy hungry eyes, even till they wink with fulness,
Tomorrow see again, and do not kill
The spirit of Love, with a perpetual dulness:
Let this sad interim like the Ocean be
Which parts the shore, where two contracted new,
Come daily to the banks, that when they see
Return of love, more blest may be the view.
 Or call it Winter, which being full of care,
  Makes Summer's welcome, thrice more wish'd, more rare.

57

Being your slave what should I do but tend
Upon the hours, and times of your desire?
I have no precious time at all to spend;
Nor services to do till you require.
Nor dare I chide the world without end hour,
Whilst I (my sovereign) watch the clock for you,
Nor think the bitterness of absence sour,
When you have bid your servant once adieu.
Nor dare I question with my jealous thought,
Where you may be, or your affairs suppose,
But like a sad slave stay and think of nought
Save where you are, how happy you make those.
  So true a fool is love, that in your Will
  (Though you do anything), he thinks no ill.

58

That God forbid, that made me first your slave,
I should in thought control your times of pleasure,
Or at your hand th' account of hours to crave,
Being your vassal bound to stay your leisure.
Oh let me suffer (being at your beck)
Th' imprison'd absence of your liberty,
And patience tame, to sufferance bide each check,
Without accusing you of injury.
Be where you list, your charter is so strong,
That you yourself may privilege your time
To what you will, to you it doth belong,
Yourself to pardon of self-doing crime.
  I am to wait, though waiting so be hell,
  Not blame your pleasure be it ill or well.

59

If there be nothing new, but that which is,
Hath been before, how are our brains beguil'd,
Which labouring for invention bear amiss
The second burthen of a former child?
Oh that record could with a backward look,
Even of five hundred courses of the Sun,
Show me your image in some antique book,
Since mind at first in character was done.
That I might see what the old world could say,
To this composed wonder of your frame,
Whether we are mended, or where better they,
Or whether revolution be the same.
   Oh sure I am the wits of former days,
    To subjects worse have given admiring praise.

60

Like as the waves make towards the pebbled shore,
So do our minutes hasten to their end,
Each changing place with that which goes before,
In sequent toil all forwards do contend.
Nativity once in the main of light,
Crawls to maturity, wherewith being crown'd,
Crooked eclipses 'gainst his glory fight,
And Time that gave, doth now his gift confound.
Time doth transfix the flourish set on youth,
And delves the parallels in beauty's brow,
Feeds on the rarities of nature's truth,
And nothing stands but for his scythe to mow.
   And yet to times in hope, my verse shall stand
    Praising thy worth, despite his cruel hand.

61

Is it thy will, thy Image should keep open
My heavy eyelids to the weary night?
Dost thou desire my slumbers should be broken,
While shadows like to thee do mock my sight?
Is it thy spirit that thou send'st from thee
So far from home into my deeds to pry,
To find out shames and idle hours in me,
The scope and tenure of thy jealousy?
O no, thy love though much, is not so great,
It is my love that keeps mine eye awake,
Mine own true love that doth my rest defeat,
To play the watchman ever for thy sake.
    For thee watch I, whilst thou dost wake elsewhere,
    From me far off, with others all too near.

62

Sin of self-love possesseth all mine eye,
And all my soul, and all my every part;
And for this sin there is no remedy,
It is so grounded inward in my heart.
Methinks no face so gracious is as mine,
No shape so true, no truth of such account,
And for myself mine own worth do define,
As I all other in all worths surmount.
But when my glass shows me myself indeed,
Beated and chopp'd with tann'd antiquity,
Mine own self-love quite contrary I read;
Self, so self-loving were iniquity.
    'T is thee (my self) that for myself I praise,
    Painting my age with beauty of thy days.

63

Against my love shall be as I am now
With Time's injurious hand crush'd and o'erworn,
When hours have drain'd his blood and fill'd his brow
With lines and wrinkles, when his youthful morn
Hath travell'd on to Age's steepy night,
And all those beauties whereof now he's King
Are vanishing, or vanish'd out of sight,
Stealing away the treasure of his Spring.
For such a time do I now fortify
Against confounding Age's cruel knife,
That he shall never cut from memory
My sweet love's beauty, though my lover's life.
*   His beauty shall in these black lines be seen,*
*   And they shall live, and he in them still green.*

64

When I have seen by Time's fell hand defaced
The rich proud cost of outworn buried age.
When sometime lofty towers I see down rased,
And brass eternal slave to mortal rage.
When I have seen the hungry Ocean gain
Advantage on the kingdom of the shore,
And the firm soil win of the wat'ry main,
Increasing store with loss, and loss with store.
When I have seen such interchange of state,
Or state itself confounded, to decay,
Ruin hath taught me thus to ruminate
That Time will come and take my love away.
*   This thought is as a death which cannot choose*
*   But weep to have, that which it fears to lose.*

65

Since brass, nor stone, nor earth, nor boundless sea,
But sad mortality o'ersways their power,
How with this rage shall beauty hold a plea,
Whose action is no stronger than a flower?
O how shall summer's honey breath hold out,
Against the wrackful siege of batt'ring days,
When rocks impregnable are not so stout,
Nor gates of steel so strong but Time decays?
O fearful meditation, where alack,
Shall Time's best jewel from Time's chest lie hid?
Or what strong hand can hold his swift foot back,
Or who his spoil of beauty can forbid?
   O none, unless this miracle have might,
   That in black ink my love may still shine bright.

66

Tir'd with all these for restful death I cry,
As to behold Desert a beggar born,
And needy Nothing trimm'd in jollity,
And purest Faith unhappily forsworn,
And gilded Honour shamefully misplac'd,
And maiden Virtue rudely strumpeted,
And right Perfection wrongfully disgrac'd,
And Strength by limping sway disabled,
And Art made tongue-tied by Authority,
And Folly (doctor-like) controlling Skill,
And simple Truth miscall'd Simplicity,
And captive Good attending Captain Ill.
   Tir'd with all these, from these would I be gone,
   Save that to die, I leave my love alone.

67

Ah wherefore with infection should he live,
And with his presence grace impiety,
That sin by him advantage should achieve,
And lace itself with his society?
Why should false painting imitate his cheek,
And steal dead seeing of his living hue?
Why should poor beauty indirectly seek
Roses of shadow, since his rose is true?
Why should he live, now Nature bankrout is,
Beggar'd of blood to blush through lively veins,
For she hath no exchequer now but his,
And proud of many, lives upon his gains?
  O him she stores, to show what wealth she had,
  In days long since, before these last so bad.

68

Thus in his cheek the map of days outworn,
When beauty liv'd and died as flowers do now,
Before these bastard signs of fair were borne,
Or durst inhabit on a living brow:
Before the golden tresses of the dead,
The right of sepulchres, were shorn away,
To live a second life on second head,
Ere beauty's dead fleece made another gay:
In him those holy antique hours are seen,
Without all ornament, itself and true,
Making no summer of another's green,
Robbing no old to dress his beauty new,
  And him as for a map doth Nature store,
  To show false Art what beauty was of yore.

69

Those parts of thee that the world's eye doth view,
Want nothing that the thought of hearts can mend:
All tongues (the voice of souls) give thee that due,
Utt'ring bare truth, even so as foes commend.
Thine outward thus with outward praise is crown'd,
But those same tongues that give thee so thine own,
In other accents do this praise confound
By seeing farther than the eye hath shown.
They look into the beauty of thy mind,
And that in guess they measure by thy deeds,
Then churls their thoughts (although their eyes were kind)
To thy fair flower add the rank smell of weeds,
  But why thy odour matcheth not thy show,
  The soil is this, that thou dost common grow.

70

That thou art blam'd shall not be thy defect,
For slander's mark was ever yet the fair,
The ornament of beauty is suspect,
A crow that flies in heaven's sweetest air.
So thou be good, slander doth but approve,
Thy worth the greater being woo'd of time,
For canker vice the sweetest buds doth love,
And thou present'st a pure unstained prime.
Thou hast pass'd by the ambush of young days,
Either not assail'd, or victor being charg'd,
Yet this thy praise cannot be so thy praise,
To tie up envy, evermore enlarg'd:
  If some suspect of ill mask'd not thy show,
  Then thou alone kingdoms of hearts shouldst owe.

71

No longer mourn for me when I am dead,
Than you shall hear the surly sullen bell
Give warning to the world that I am fled
From this vile world with vilest worms to dwell:
Nay if you read this line, remember not
The hand that writ it, for I love you so,
That I in your sweet thoughts would be forgot,
If thinking on me then should make you woe.
O if (I say) you look upon this verse,
When I (perhaps) compounded am with clay,
Do not so much as my poor name rehearse;
But let your love even with my life decay.
　　Lest the wise world should look into your moan,
　　And mock you with me after I am gone.

72

O lest the world should task you to recite,
What merit liv'd in me that you should love
After my death (dear love) forget me quite,
For you in me can nothing worthy prove.
Unless you would devise some virtuous lie,
To do more for me than mine own desert,
And hang more praise upon deceased I,
Than niggard truth would willingly impart:
O lest your true love may seem false in this,
That you for love speak well of me untrue,
My name be buried where my body is,
And live no more to shame nor me, nor you.
　　For I am sham'd by that which I bring forth,
　　And so should you, to love things nothing worth.

73

That time of year thou mayst in me behold,
When yellow leaves, or none, or few do hang
Upon those boughs which shake against the cold,
Bare ruin'd choirs, where late the sweet birds sang.
In me thou seest the twilight of such day,
As after sunset fadeth in the West,
Which by and by black night doth take away,
Death's second self that seals up all in rest.
In me thou seest the glowing of such fire,
That on the ashes of his youth doth lie,
As the death-bed, whereon it must expire,
Consum'd with that which it was nourish'd by.
    This thou perceiv'st, which makes thy love more strong,
    To love that well, which thou must leave ere long.

74

But be contented when that fell arrest,
Without all bail shall carry me away,
My life hath in this line some interest,
Which for memorial still with thee shall stay.
When thou reviewest this, thou dost review,
The very part was consecrate to thee,
The earth can have but earth, which is his due,
My spirit is thine the better part of me.
So then thou hast but lost the dregs of life,
The prey of worms, my body being dead,
The coward conquest of a wretch's knife,
Too base of thee to be remembered.
    The worth of that, is that which it contains,
    And that is this, and this with thee remains.

75

So are you to my thoughts as food to life,
Or as sweet-season'd showers are to the ground;
And for the peace of you I hold such strife,
As 'twixt a miser and his wealth is found.
Now proud as an enjoyer, and anon
Doubting the filching age will steal his treasure,
Now counting best to be with you alone,
Then better'd that the world may see my pleasure.
Sometime all full with feasting on your sight,
And by and by clean starved for a look,
Possessing or pursuing no delight
Save what is had, or must from you be took.
   Thus do I pine and surfeit day by day,
   Or gluttoning on all, or all away.

76

Why is my verse so barren of new pride?
So far from variation or quick change?
Why with the time do I not glance aside
To new found methods, and to compounds strange?
Why write I still all one, ever the same,
And keep invention in a noted weed,
That every word doth almost tell my name,
Showing their birth, and where they did proceed?
O know sweet love I always write of you,
And you and love are still my argument:
So all my best is dressing old words new,
Spending again what is already spent:
   For as the Sun is daily new and old,
   So is my love still telling what is told.

77

Thy glass will show thee how thy beauties wear,
Thy dial how thy precious minutes waste,
The vacant leaves thy mind's imprint will bear,
And of this book, this learning mayst thou taste.
The wrinkles which thy glass will truly show,
Of mouthed graves will give thee memory,
Thou by thy dial's shady stealth mayst know,
Time's thievish progress to eternity.
Look what thy memory cannot contain,
Commit to these waste blanks, and thou shalt find
Those children nurs'd, deliver'd from thy brain,
To take a new acquaintance of thy mind.
    These offices, so oft as thou wilt look,
     Shall profit thee, and much enrich thy book.

78

So oft have I invok'd thee for my Muse,
And found such fair assistance in my verse,
As every alien pen hath got my use,
And under thee their poesy disperse.
Thine eyes, that taught the dumb on high to sing,
And heavy ignorance aloft to fly,
Have added feathers to the learned's wing,
And given grace a double majesty.
Yet be most proud of that which I compile,
Whose influence is thine, and born of thee,
In others' works thou dost but mend the style,
And arts with thy sweet graces graced be.
    But thou art all my art, and dost advance
     As high as learning, my rude ignorance.

79

Whilst I alone did call upon thy aid,
My verse alone had all thy gentle grace,
But now my gracious numbers are decay'd,
And my sick Muse doth give another place.
I grant (sweet love) thy lovely argument
Deserves the travail of a worthier pen,
Yet what of thee thy Poet doth invent,
He robs thee of, and pays it thee again,
He lends thee virtue, and he stole that word,
From thy behaviour, beauty doth he give
And found it in thy cheek: he can afford
No praise to thee, but what in thee doth live.
    Then thank him not for that which he doth say,
    Since what he owes thee, thou thyself dost pay.

80

O how I faint when I of you do write,
Knowing a better spirit doth use your name,
And in the praise thereof spends all his might,
To make me tongue-tied speaking of your fame.
But since your worth (wide as the Ocean is)
The humble as the proudest sail doth bear,
My saucy bark (inferior far to his)
On your broad main doth wilfully appear.
Your shallowest help will hold me up afloat,
Whilst he upon your soundless deep doth ride,
Or (being wrack'd) I am a worthless boat,
He of tall building, and of goodly pride.
    Then if he thrive and I be cast away,
    The worst was this, my love was my decay.

81

Or I shall live your Epitaph to make,
Or you survive when I in earth am rotten,
From hence your memory death cannot take,
Although in me each part will be forgotten.
Your name from hence immortal life shall have,
Though I (once gone) to all the world must die,
The earth can yield me but a common grave,
When you entombed in men's eyes shall lie.
Your monument shall be my gentle verse,
Which eyes not yet created shall o'er-read,
And tongues to be, your being shall rehearse,
When all the breathers of this world are dead,
    You still shall live (such virtue hath my pen)
    Where breath most breathes, even in the mouths of men.

82

I grant thou wert not married to my Muse,
And therefore mayst without attaint o'erlook
The dedicated words which writers use
Of their fair subject, blessing every book.
Thou art as fair in knowledge as in hue,
Finding thy worth a limit past my praise,
And therefore art enforc'd to seek anew,
Some fresher stamp of the time-bettering days.
And do so love, yet when they have devis'd,
What strained touches Rhetoric can lend,
Thou truly fair, wert truly sympathis'd,
In true plain words, by thy true-telling friend.
    And their gross painting might be better us'd,
    Where cheeks need blood, in thee it is abus'd.

83

I never saw that you did painting need,
And therefore to your fair no painting set,
I found (or thought I found) you did exceed
The barren tender of a Poet's debt:
And therefore have I slept in your report,
That you yourself being extant well might show,
How far a modern quill doth come too short,
Speaking of worth, what worth in you doth grow.
This silence for my sin you did impute,
Which shall be most my glory being dumb,
For I impair not beauty being mute,
When others would give life, and bring a tomb.
    There lives more life in one of your fair eyes,
    Than both your Poets can in praise devise.

84

Who is it that says most, which can say more,
Than this rich praise, that you alone, are you,
In whose confine immured is the store,
Which should example where your equal grew?
Lean penury within that pen doth dwell,
That to his subject lends not some small glory,
But he that writes of you, if he can tell,
That you are you, so dignifies his story.
Let him but copy what in you is writ,
Not making worse what nature made so clear,
And such a counterpart shall fame his wit,
Making his style admired everywhere.
    You to your beauteous blessings add a curse,
    Being fond on praise, which makes your praises worse.

85

My tongue-tied Muse in manners holds her still,
While comments of your praise richly compil'd,
Reserve their character with golden quill,
And precious phrase by all the Muses fil'd.
I think good thoughts, while others write good words,
And like unlettered clerk still cry Amen,
To every Hymn that able spirit affords,
In polish'd form of well refined pen.
Hearing you prais'd, I say 't is so, 't is true,
And to the most of praise add something more,
But that is in my thought, whose love to you
(Though words come hindmost) holds his rank before.
 Then others, for the breath of words respect,
 Me for my dumb thoughts, speaking in effect.

86

Was it the proud full sail of his great verse,
Bound for the prize of (all too precious) you,
That did my ripe thoughts in my brain inhearse,
Making their tomb the womb wherein they grew?
Was it his spirit, by spirits taught to write,
Above a mortal pitch, that struck me dead?
No, neither he, nor his compeers by night
Giving him aid, my verse astonished.
He nor that affable familiar ghost
Which nightly gulls him with intelligence,
As victors of my silence cannot boast,
I was not sick of any fear from thence.
 But when your countenance fill'd up his line,
 Then lack'd I matter, that enfeebled mine.

87

Farewell thou art too dear for my possessing,
And like enough thou know'st thy estimate,
The charter of thy worth gives thee releasing:
My bonds in thee are all determinate.
For how do I hold thee but by thy granting,
And for that riches where is my deserving?
The cause of this fair gift in me is wanting,
And so my patent back again is swerving.
Thyself thou gav'st, thy own worth then not knowing,
Or me to whom thou gav'st it, else mistaking,
So thy great gift upon misprision growing,
Comes home again, on better judgment making.
Thus have I had thee as a dream doth flatter,
In sleep a King, but waking no such matter.

88

When thou shalt be dispos'd to set me light,
And place my merit in the eye of scorn,
Upon thy side, against myself I'll fight,
And prove thee virtuous, though thou art forsworn:
With mine own weakness being best acquainted,
Upon thy part I can set down a story
Of faults conceal'd, wherein I am attainted:
That thou in losing me, shalt win much glory:
And I by this will be a gainer too,
For bending all my loving thoughts on thee,
The injuries that to myself I do,
Doing thee vantage, double vantage me.
Such is my love, to thee I so belong,
That for thy right, myself will bear all wrong.

89

Say that thou didst forsake me for some fault,
And I will comment upon that offence,
Speak of my lameness, and I straight will halt:
Against thy reasons making no defence.
Thou canst not (love) disgrace me half so ill,
To set a form upon desired change,
As I'll myself disgrace, knowing thy will,
I will acquaintance strangle and look strange:
Be absent from thy walks and in my tongue,
Thy sweet-beloved name no more shall dwell,
Lest I (too much profane) should do it wrong:
And haply of our old acquaintance tell.
    For thee, against myself I'll vow debate,
    For I must ne'er love him whom thou dost hate.

90

Then hate me when thou wilt, if ever, now,
Now while the world is bent my deeds to cross,
Join with the spite of fortune, make me bow,
And do not drop in for an after-loss:
Ah do not, when my heart hath scap'd this sorrow,
Come in the rearward of a conquer'd woe,
Give not a windy night a rainy morrow,
To linger out a purpos'd overthrow.
If thou wilt leave me, do not leave me last,
When other petty griefs have done their spite,
But in the onset come, so shall I taste
At first the very worst of fortune's might.
    And other strains of woe, which now seem woe,
    Compar'd with loss of thee, will not seem so.

91

Some glory in their birth, some in their skill,
Some in their wealth, some in their body's force,
Some in their garments though new-fangled ill:
Some in their hawks and hounds, some in their horse.
And every humour hath his adjunct pleasure,
Wherein it finds a joy above the rest,
But these particulars are not my measure,
All these I better in one general best.
Thy love is better than high birth to me,
Richer than wealth, prouder than garments' cost,
Of more delight than hawks or horses be:
And having thee, of all men's pride I boast.
   Wretched in this alone, that thou mayst take
   All this away, and me most wretched make.

92

But do thy worst to steal thyself away,
For term of life thou art assured mine,
And life no longer than thy love will stay,
For it depends upon that love of thine.
Then need I not to fear the worst of wrongs,
When in the least of them my life hath end,
I see a better state to me belongs
Than that, which on thy humour doth depend.
Thou canst not vex me with inconstant mind,
Since that my life on thy revolt doth lie,
Oh what a happy title do I find,
Happy to have thy love, happy to die!
   But what's so blessed fair that fears no blot,
   Thou mayst be false, and yet I know it not.

93

So shall I live, supposing thou art true,
Like a deceived husband, so love's face,
May still seem love to me, though alter'd-new:
Thy looks with me, thy heart in other place.
For there can live no hatred in thine eye,
Therefore in that I cannot know thy change,
In many's looks, the false heart's history
Is writ in moods and frowns and wrinkles strange.
But heaven in thy creation did decree,
That in thy face sweet love should ever dwell,
Whate'er thy thoughts, or thy heart's workings be,
Thy looks should nothing thence, but sweetness tell.
    How like Eve's apple doth thy beauty grow,
    If thy sweet virtue answer not thy show.

94

They that have power to hurt, and will do none,
That do not do the thing they most do show,
Who moving others, are themselves as stone,
Unmoved, cold, and to temptation slow:
They rightly do inherit heaven's graces,
And husband nature's riches from expense,
They are the Lords and owners of their faces,
Others, but stewards of their excellence:
The summer's flower is to the summer sweet,
Though to itself, it only live and die,
But if that flower with base infection meet,
The basest weed outbraves his dignity:
    For sweetest things turn sourest by their deeds,
    Lilies that fester, smell far worse than weeds.

95

How sweet and lovely dost thou make the shame,
Which like a canker in the fragrant rose,
Doth spot the beauty of thy budding name!
Oh in what sweets dost thou thy sins enclose!
That tongue that tells the story of thy days
(Making lascivious comments on thy sport),
Cannot dispraise, but in a kind of praise,
Naming thy name, blesses an ill report.
Oh what a mansion have those vices got,
Which for their habitation chose out thee,
Where beauty's veil doth cover every blot,
And all things turns to fair, that eyes can see!
　　Take heed (dear heart) of this large privilege,
　　The hardest knife ill-us'd doth lose his edge.

96

Some say thy fault is youth, some wantonness,
Some say thy grace is youth and gentle sport,
Both grace and faults are lov'd of more and less:
Thou mak'st faults graces, that to thee resort:
As on the finger of a throned Queen,
The basest jewel will be well esteem'd:
So are those errors that in thee are seen,
To truths translated, and for true things deem'd.
How many lambs might the stern wolf betray,
If like a lamb he could his looks translate.
How many gazers mightst thou lead away,
If thou wouldst use the strength of all thy state!
　　But do not so, I love thee in such sort,
　　As thou being mine, mine is thy good report.

97

How like a Winter hath my absence been
From thee, the pleasure of the fleeting year!
What freezings have I felt, what dark days seen?
What old December's bareness everywhere?
And yet this time remov'd was summer's time,
The teeming Autumn big with rich increase,
Bearing the wanton burthen of the prime,
Like widowed wombs after their Lords' decease:
Yet this abundant issue seem'd to me,
But hope of orphans, and unfathered fruit,
For Summer and his pleasures wait on thee,
And thou away, the very birds are mute.
　　Or if they sing, 't is with so dull a cheer,
　　That leaves look pale, dreading the Winter's near.

98

From you have I been absent in the spring,
When proud pied April (dress'd in all his trim)
Hath put a spirit of youth in everything:
That heavy Saturn laugh'd and leap'd with him.
Yet nor the lays of birds, nor the sweet smell
Of different flowers in odour and in hue,
Could make me any summer's story tell:
Or from their proud lap pluck them where they grew:
Nor did I wonder at the lilies white,
Nor praise the deep vermilion in the rose,
They were but sweet, but figures of delight:
Drawn after you, you pattern of all those.
　　Yet seem'd it Winter still, and you away,
　　As with your shadow I with these did play.

99

The forward violet thus did I chide,
Sweet thief whence didst thou steal thy sweet that smells,
If not from my love's breath? the purple pride,
Which on thy soft cheek for complexion dwells
In my love's veins thou hast too grossly dy'd.
The lily I condemned for thy hand,
And buds of marjoram had stolen thy hair,
The roses fearfully on thorns did stand,
One blushing shame, another white despair:
A third nor red, nor white, had stolen of both,
And to his robb'ry had annex'd thy breath,
But for his theft in pride of all his growth
A vengeful canker eat him up to death.
　More flowers I noted, yet I none could see,
　But sweet, or colour it had stolen from thee.

100

Where art thou Muse that thou forgett'st so long,
To speak of that which gives thee all thy might?
Spend'st thou thy fury on some worthless song,
Dark'ning thy power to lend base subjects light?
Return forgetful Muse, and straight redeem,
In gentle numbers time so idly spent,
Sing to the ear that doth thy lays esteem,
And gives thy pen both skill and argument.
Rise resty Muse, my love's sweet face survey,
If Time have any wrinkle graven there,
If any, be a satire to decay,
And make Time's spoils despised everywhere.
　Give my love fame faster than time wastes life,
　So thou prevent'st his scythe, and crooked knife.

101

Oh truant Muse, what shall be thy amends,
For thy neglect of truth in beauty dy'd?
Both truth and beauty on my love depends:
So dost thou too, and therein dignifi'd:
Make answer Muse, wilt thou not haply say,
Truth needs no colour with his colour fix'd,
Beauty no pencil, beauty's truth to lay:
But best is best, if never intermix'd.
Because he needs no praise, wilt thou be dumb?
Excuse not silence so, for 't lies in thee,
To make him much outlive a gilded tomb:
And to be prais'd of ages yet to be.
    Then do thy office Muse, I teach thee how,
    To make him seem long hence, as he shows now.

102

My love is strengthen'd though more weak in seeming,
I love not less, though less the show appear,
That love is merchandis'd, whose rich esteeming,
The owner's tongue doth publish everywhere.
Our love was new, and then but in the spring,
When I was wont to greet it with my lays,
As Philomel in summer's front doth sing,
And stops her pipe in growth of riper days:
Not that the summer is less pleasant now
Than when her mournful hymns did hush the night,
But that wild music burthens every bough,
And sweets grown common lose their dear delight.
    Therefore like her, I sometime hold my tongue:
    Because I would not dull you with my song.

103

Alack what poverty my Muse brings forth,
That having such a scope to show her pride,
The argument all bare is of more worth
Than when it hath my added praise beside.
Oh blame me not if I no more can write!
Look in your glass and there appears a face,
That over-goes my blunt invention quite,
Dulling my lines, and doing me disgrace.
Were it not sinful then striving to mend,
To mar the subject that before was well,
For to no other pass my verses tend,
Than of your graces and your gifts to tell.
　　And more, much more than in my verse can sit,
　　Your own glass shows you, when you look in it.

104

To me fair friend you never can be old,
For as you were when first your eye I eyed,
Such seems your beauty still: three Winters' cold,
Have from the forests shook three Summers' pride,
Three beauteous springs to yellow Autumn turn'd,
In process of the seasons have I seen,
Three April perfumes in three hot Junes burn'd,
Since first I saw you fresh which yet are green.
Ah yet doth beauty like a dial hand,
Steal from his figure, and no pace perceiv'd,
So your sweet hue, which methinks still doth stand,
Hath motion, and mine eye may be deceiv'd.
　　For fear of which, hear this thou age unbred,
　　Ere you were born was beauty's summer dead.

105

Let not my love be call'd idolatry,
Nor my beloved as an idol show,
Since all alike my songs and praises be
To one, of one, still such, and ever so.
Kind is my love today, tomorrow kind,
Still constant in a wondrous excellence,
Therefore my verse to constancy confin'd,
One thing expressing, leaves out difference.
Fair, kind, and true, is all my argument,
Fair, kind and true, varying to other words,
And in this change is my invention spent,
Three themes in one, which wondrous scope affords.
    Fair, kind, and true, have often liv'd alone,
    Which three till now, never kept seat in one.

106

When in the Chronicle of wasted time,
I see descriptions of the fairest wights,
And beauty making beautiful old rhyme,
In praise of Ladies dead, and lovely Knights,
Then in the blazon of sweet beauty's best,
Of hand, of foot, of lip, of eye, of brow,
I see their antique pen would have express'd,
Even such a beauty as you master now.
So all their praises are but prophecies
Of this our time, all you prefiguring,
And for they look'd but with divining eyes,
They had not skill enough your worth to sing:
    For we which now behold these present days,
    Have eyes to wonder, but lack tongues to praise.

107

Not mine own fears, nor the prophetic soul,
Of the wide world, dreaming on things to come,
Can yet the lease of my true love control,
Suppos'd as forfeit to a confin'd doom.
The mortal Moon hath her eclipse endur'd,
And the sad Augurs mock their own presage,
Incertainties now crown themselves assur'd,
And peace proclaims olives of endless age.
Now with the drops of this most balmy time,
My love looks fresh, and Death to me subscribes,
Since spite of him I 'll live in this poor rhyme,
While he insults o'er dull and speechless tribes.
    And thou in this shalt find thy monument,
        When tyrants' crests and tombs of brass are spent.

108

What 's in the brain that ink may character,
Which hath not figur'd to thee my true spirit,
What 's new to speak, what new to register,
That may express my love, or thy dear merit?
Nothing sweet boy, but yet like prayers divine,
I must each day say o'er the very same,
Counting no old thing old, thou mine, I thine,
Even as when first I hallowed thy fair name.
So that eternal love in love's fresh case,
Weighs not the dust and injury of age,
Nor gives to necessary wrinkles place,
But makes antiquity for aye his page,
    Finding the first conceit of love there bred,
        Where time and outward form would show **it dead**.

109

O never say that I was false of heart,
Though absence seem'd my flame to qualify,
As easy might I from myself depart,
As from my soul which in thy breast doth lie:
That is my home of love, if I have rang'd,
Like him that travels I return again,
Just to the time, not with the time exchang'd,
So that myself bring water for my stain:
Never believe though in my nature reign'd,
All frailties that besiege all kinds of blood,
That it could so preposterously be stain'd,
To leave for nothing all thy sum of good:
    For nothing this wide Universe I call,
    Save thou my Rose, in it thou art my all.

110

Alas 't is true, I have gone here and there,
And made myself a motley to the view,
Gor'd mine own thoughts, sold cheap what is most dear,
Made old offences of affections new.
Most true it is, that I have look'd on truth
Askance and strangely: but by all above,
These blenches gave my heart another youth,
And worse essays prov'd thee my best of love.
Now all is done, have what shall have no end,
Mine appetite I never more will grind
On newer proof, to try an older friend,
A God in love, to whom I am confin'd.
    Then give me welcome, next my heaven the best,
    Even to thy pure and most, most loving breast.

III

O for my sake do you with Fortune chide,
The guilty goddess of my harmful deeds,
That did not better for my life provide,
Than public means which public manners breeds.
Thence comes it that my name receives a brand,
And almost thence my nature is subdu'd
To what it works in, like the dyer's hand:
Pity me then, and wish I were renew'd,
Whilst like a willing patient I will drink,
Potions of eysell 'gainst my strong infection,
No bitterness that I will bitter think,
Nor double penance to correct correction.
    Pity me then dear friend, and I assure ye,
    Even that your pity is enough to cure me.

112

Your love and pity doth th' impression fill,
Which vulgar scandal stamp'd upon my brow,
For what care I who calls me well or ill,
So you o'er-green my bad, my good allow?
You are my All the world, and I must strive,
To know my shames and praises from your tongue,
None else to me, nor I to none alive,
That my steel'd sense or changes right or wrong.
In so profound abysm I throw all care
Of other's voices, that my adder's sense,
To critic and to flatterer stopped are:
Mark how with my neglect I do dispense.
    You are so strongly in my purpose bred,
    That all the world besides me thinks y' are dead.

113

Since I left you, mine eye is in my mind,
And that which governs me to go about,
Doth part his function, and is partly blind,
Seems seeing, but effectually is out:
For it no form delivers to the heart
Of bird, of flower, or shape which it doth latch,
Of his quick objects hath the mind no part,
Nor his own vision holds what it doth catch:
For if it see the rud'st or gentlest sight,
The most sweet favour or deformed'st creature,
The mountain, or the sea, the day, or night,
The crow, or dove, it shapes them to your feature.
  Incapable of more, replete with you,
    My most true mind thus maketh mine untrue.

114

Or whether doth my mind being crown'd with you
Drink up the monarch's plague this flattery?
Or whether shall I say mine eye saith true,
And that your love taught it this Alchymy?
To make of monsters, and things indigest,
Such cherubins as your sweet self resemble,
Creating every bad a perfect best
As fast as objects to his beams assemble:
Oh 't is the first, 't is flatt'ry in my seeing,
And my great mind most kingly drinks it up,
Mine eye well knows what with his gust is 'greeing,
And to his palate doth prepare the cup.
  If it be poison'd, 't is the lesser sin,
    That mine eye loves it and doth first begin.

115

Those lines that I before have writ do lie,
Even those that said I could not love you dearer,
Yet then my judgment knew no reason why,
My most full flame should afterwards burn clearer.
But reckoning time, whose million'd accidents
Creep in 'twixt vows, and change decrees of Kings,
Tan sacred beauty, blunt the sharp'st intents,
Divert strong minds to th' course of alt'ring things:
Alas why fearing of Time's tyranny,
Might I not then say now I love you best,
When I was certain o'er incertainty,
Crowning the present, doubting of the rest:
    Love is a babe, then might I not say so
    To give full growth to that which still doth grow.

116

Let me not to the marriage of true minds
Admit impediments, love is not love
Which alters when it alteration finds,
Or bends with the remover to remove.
O no, it is an ever-fixed mark
That looks on tempest and is never shaken;
It is the star to every wand'ring bark,
Whose worth's unknown, although his height be taken,
Love's not Time's fool, though rosy lips and cheeks
Within his bending sickle's compass come,
Love alters not with his brief hours and weeks,
But bears it out even to the edge of doom:
    If this be error and upon me proved,
    I never writ, nor no man ever loved.

117

Accuse me thus, that I have scanted all,
Wherein I should your great deserts repay,
Forgot upon your dearest love to call,
Whereto all bonds do tie me day by day,
That I have frequent been with unknown minds,
And given to time your own dear purchas'd right,
That I have hoisted sail to all the winds
Which should transport me farthest from your sight.
Book both my wilfulness and errors down,
And on just proof surmise, accumulate,
Bring me within the level of your frown,
But shoot not at me in your wakened hate:
    Since my appeal says I did strive to prove
    The constancy and virtue of your love.

118

Like as to make our appetites more keen
With eager compounds we our palate urge,
As to prevent our maladies unseen,
We sicken to shun sickness when we purge.
Even so being full of your ne'er cloying sweetness,
To bitter sauces did I frame my feeding;
And sick of welfare found a kind of meetness,
To be diseas'd ere that there was true needing.
Thus policy in love t' anticipate
The ills that were not, grew to faults assured,
And brought to medicine a healthful state
Which rank of goodness would by ill be cured.
    But thence I learn and find the lesson true,
    Drugs poison him that so fell sick of you.

119

What potions have I drunk of Siren tears
Distill'd from limbecks foul as hell within,
Applying fears to hopes, and hopes to fears,
Still losing when I saw myself to win?
What wretched errors hath my heart committed,
Whilst it hath thought itself so blessed never?
How have mine eyes out of their spheres been fitted
In the distraction of this madding fever?
O benefit of ill, now I find true
That better is, by evil still made better.
And ruin'd love when it is built anew
Grows fairer than at first, more strong, far greater.
   So I return rebuk'd to my content,
    And gain by ills thrice more than I have spent.

120

That you were once unkind befriends me now,
And for that sorrow, which I then did feel,
Needs must I under my transgression bow,
Unless my nerves were brass or hammered steel.
For if you were by my unkindness shaken,
As I by yours, y' have pass'd a hell of Time,
And I a tyrant have no leisure taken
To weigh how once I suffered in your crime.
O that our night of woe might have remember'd
My deepest sense, how hard true sorrow hits,
And soon to you, as you to me then tender'd
The humble salve, which wounded bosoms fits!
   But that your trespass now becomes a fee,
    Mine ransoms yours, and yours must ransom me.

121

'Tis better to be vile than vile esteemed,
When not to be, receives reproach of being,
And the just pleasure lost, which is so deemed,
Not by our feeling, but by others' seeing.
For why should others' false adulterate eyes
Give salutation to my sportive blood?
Or on my frailties why are frailer spies,
Which in their wills count bad what I think good?
No, I am that I am, and they that level
At my abuses, reckon up their own,
I may be straight though they themselves be bevel;
By their rank thoughts, my deeds must not be shown.
　　Unless this general evil they maintain,
　　All men are bad and in their badness reign.

122

Thy gift, thy tables, are within my brain
Full character'd with lasting memory,
Which shall above that idle rank remain
Beyond all date even to eternity.
Or at the least, so long as brain and heart
Have faculty by nature to subsist,
Till each to ras'd oblivion yield his part
Of thee, thy record never can be miss'd:
That poor retention could not so much hold,
Nor need I tallies thy dear love to score,
Therefore to give them from me was I bold,
To trust those tables that receive thee more.
　　To keep an adjunct to remember thee,
　　Were to import forgetfulness in me.

123

No! Time, thou shalt not boast that I do change,
Thy pyramids built up with newer might
To me are nothing novel, nothing strange,
They are but dressings of a former sight:
Our dates are brief, and therefore we admire,
What thou dost foist upon us that is old,
And rather make them born to our desire,
Than think that we before have heard them told:
Thy registers and thee I both defy,
Not wond'ring at the present, nor the past,
For thy records, and what we see doth lie,
Made more or less by thy continual haste:
    This I do vow and this shall ever be,
    I will be true despite thy scythe and thee.

124

If my dear love were but the child of state,
It might for Fortune's bastard be unfathered,
As subject to Time's love, or to Time's hate,
Weeds among weeds, or flowers with flowers gathered.
No it was builded far from accident,
It suffers not in smiling pomp, nor falls
Under the blow of thralled discontent,
Whereto th' inviting time our fashion calls:
It fears not policy that heretic,
Which works on leases of short number'd hours,
But all alone stands hugely politic,
That it nor grows with heat, nor drowns with showers.
    To this I witness call the fools of Time,
    Which die for goodness, who have liv'd for crime.

125

Were 't aught to me I bore the canopy,
With my extern the outward honouring,
Or laid great bases for eternity,
Which proves more short than waste or ruining?
Have I not seen dwellers on form and favour
Lose all, and more by paying too much rent.
For compound sweet; foregoing simple savour,
Pitiful thrivers in their gazing spent.
No, let me be obsequious in thy heart,
And take thou my oblation, poor but free,
Which is not mix'd with seconds, knows no art,
But mutual render only me for thee.
*   Hence, thou suborn'd Informer, a true soul*
*   When most impeach'd, stands least in thy control.*

126

O thou my lovely Boy who in thy power,
Dost hold Time's fickle glass, his sickle, hour:
Who hast by waning grown, and therein show'st,
Thy lovers withering, as thy sweet self grow'st.
If Nature (sovereign mistress over wrack)
As thou goest onwards still will pluck thee back,
She keeps thee to this purpose, that her skill
May Time disgrace, and wretched minute kill.
Yet fear her O thou minion of her pleasure,
She may detain, but not still keep her treasure!
Her audit (though delay'd) answer'd must be,
And her quietus is to render thee.
*   (   )*
*   (   )*

127

In the old age black was not counted fair,
Or if it were it bore not beauty's name:
But now is black Beauty's successive heir,
And Beauty slander'd with a bastard shame,
For since each hand hath put on Nature's power,
Fairing the foul with Art's false borrow'd face,
Sweet Beauty hath no name, no holy bower,
But is profan'd, if not lives in disgrace.
Therefore my Mistress' eyes are raven black,
Her eyes so suited, and they mourners seem,
At such who not born fair no beauty lack,
Sland'ring Creation with a false esteem,
    Yet so they mourn becoming of their woe,
    That every tongue says Beauty should look so.

128

How oft when thou my music music play'st,
Upon that blessed wood whose motion sounds
With thy sweet fingers when thou gently sway'st,
The wiry concord that mine ear confounds,
Do I envy those jacks that nimble leap,
To kiss the tender inward of thy hand,
Whilst my poor lips which should that harvest reap,
At the wood's boldness by thee blushing stand.
To be so tickled they would change their state,
And situation with those dancing chips,
O'er whom thy fingers walk with gentle gait,
Making dead wood more bless'd than living lips:
    Since saucy jacks so happy are in this,
    Give them thy fingers, me thy lips to kiss.

129

Th' expense of Spirit in a waste of shame
Is lust in action, and till action, lust
Is perjur'd, murd'rous, bloody full of blame,
Savage, extreme, rude, cruel, not to trust,
Enjoy'd no sooner but despised straight,
Past reason hunted, and no sooner had
Past reason hated as a swallowed bait,
On purpose laid to make the taker mad.
Mad in pursuit and in possession so,
Had, having, and in quest to have, extreme,
A bliss in proof and proud and very woe,
Before a joy propos'd behind a dream,
 All this the world well knows yet none knows well,
 To shun the heaven that leads men to this hell.

130

My Mistress' eyes are nothing like the Sun,
Coral is far more red, than her lips' red,
If snow be white, why then her breasts are dun :
If hairs be wires, black wires grow on her head:
I have seen roses damask'd, red and white,
But no such roses see I in her cheeks,
And in some perfumes is there more delight,
Than in the breath that from my Mistress reeks.
I love to hear her speak, yet well I know,
That Music hath a far more pleasing sound :
I grant I never saw a goddess go,
My Mistress when she walks treads on the ground.
 And yet by heaven I think my love as rare,
 As any she beli'd with false compare.

131

Thou art as tyrannous, so as thou art,
As those whose beauties proudly make them cruel :
For well thou know'st to my dear doting heart
Thou art the fairest and most precious jewel.
Yet in good faith some say that thee behold,
Thy face hath not the power to make love groan;
To say they err, I dare not be so bold,
Although I swear it to myself alone.
And to be sure that is not false I swear
A thousand groans but thinking on thy face,
One on another's neck do witness bear
Thy black is fairest in my judgment's place.
 In nothing art thou black save in thy deeds,
 And thence this slander as I think proceeds.

132

Thine eyes I love, and they as pitying me,
Knowing thy heart torment me with disdain,
Have put on black, and loving mourners be,
Looking with pretty ruth upon my pain.
And truly not the morning Sun of Heaven
Better becomes the grey cheeks of th' East,
Nor that full Star that ushers in the Even
Doth half that glory to the sober West
As those two mourning eyes become thy face :
O let it then as well beseem thy heart
To mourn for me since mourning doth thee grace,
And suit thy pity like in every part.
 Then will I swear Beauty herself is black,
 And all they foul that thy complexion lack.

133

Beshrew that heart that makes my heart to groan
For that deep wound it gives my friend and me;
Is 't not enough to torture me alone,
But slave to slavery my sweet'st friend must be.
Me from myself thy cruel eye hath taken,
And my next self thou harder hast engrossed,
Of him, myself, and thee I am forsaken,
A torment thrice three-fold thus to be crossed:
Prison my heart in thy steel bosom's ward,
But then my friend's heart let my poor heart bail,
Who e'er keeps me, let my heart be his guard,
Thou canst not then use rigour in my jail.
    And yet thou wilt, for I being pent in thee,
    Perforce am thine and all that is in me.

134

So now I have confess'd that he is thine,
And I myself am mortgag'd to thy will,
Myself I'll forfeit, so that other mine,
Thou wilt restore to be my comfort still:
But thou wilt not, nor he will not be free,
For thou art covetous, and he is kind,
He learn'd but surety-like to write for me,
Under that bond that him as fast doth bind.
The statute of thy beauty thou wilt take,
Thou usurer that putt'st forth all to use,
And sue a friend, came debtor for my sake,
So him I lose through my unkind abuse.
    Him have I lost, thou hast both him and me,
    He pays the whole, and yet am I not free.

135

Whoever hath her wish, thou hast thy Will,
And Will to boot, and Will in over-plus,
More than enough am I that vex thee still,
To thy sweet will making addition thus.
Wilt thou whose will is large and spacious,
Not once vouchsafe to hide my will in thine,
Shall will in others seem right gracious,
And in my will no fair acceptance shine:
The sea all water, yet receives rain still,
And in abundance addeth to his store,
So thou being rich in Will add to thy Will,
One will of mine to make thy large Will more.
   Let no unkind, no fair beseechers kill,
   Think all but one, and me in that one Will.

136

If thy soul check thee that I come so near,
Swear to thy blind soul that I was thy Will,
And will thy soul knows is admitted there,
Thus far for love, my love-suit sweet fulfil.
Will, will fulfil the treasure of thy love,
Ay fill it full with wills, and my will one,
In things of great receipt with ease we prove.
Among a number one is reckon'd none.
Then in the number let me pass untold,
Though in thy stores' account I one must be,
For nothing hold me so it please thee hold,
That nothing me, a something sweet to thee.
   Make but my name thy love, and love that still,
   And then thou lov'st me for my name is Will.

137

Thou blind fool Love, what dost thou to mine eyes,
That they behold and see not what they see:
They know what beauty is, see where it lies,
Yet what the best is, take the worst to be.
If eyes corrupt by over-partial looks,
Be anchor'd in the bay where all men ride,
Why of eyes' falsehood hast thou forged hooks,
Whereto the judgment of my heart is tied?
Why should my heart think that a several plot,
Which my heart knows the wide world's common place?
Or mine eyes seeing this, say this is not
To put fair truth upon so foul a face.
  In things right true my heart and eyes have erred,
  And to this false plague are they now transferred.

138

When my love swears that she is made of truth,
I do believe her though I know she lies,
That she might think me some untutor'd youth,
Unlearned in the world's false subtleties.
Thus vainly thinking that she thinks me young,
Although she knows my days are past the best,
Simply I credit her false-speaking tongue,
On both sides thus is simple truth supprest:
But wherefore says she not she is unjust?
And wherefore say not I that I am old?
O love's best habit is in seeming trust,
And age in love, loves not t' have years told.
  Therefore I lie with her, and she with me,
  And in our faults by lies we flattered be.

139

O call not me to justify the wrong,
That thy unkindness lays upon my heart,
Wound me not with thine eye but with thy tongue,
Use power with power, and slay me not by Art,
Tell me thou lov'st elsewhere; but in my sight,
Dear heart forbear to glance thine eye aside,
What need'st thou wound with cunning when thy might
Is more than my o'erpress'd defence can bide?
Let me excuse thee, ah my love well knows,
Her pretty looks have been mine enemies,
And therefore from my face she turns my foes,
That they elsewhere might dart their injuries:
    Yet do not so, but since I am near slain,
    Kill me outright with looks, and rid my pain.

140

Be wise as thou art cruel, do not press
My tongue-tied patience with too much disdain:
Lest sorrow lend me words and words express,
The manner of my pity wanting pain.
If I might teach thee wit better it were,
Though not to love, yet love to tell me so,
As testy sick men when their deaths be near,
No news but health from their physicians know.
For if I should despair I should grow mad,
And in my madness might speak ill of thee,
Now this ill-wresting world is grown so bad,
Mad slanderers by mad ears believed be.
    That I may not be so, nor thou belied,
    Bear thine eyes straight, though thy proud heart go wide.

141

In faith I do not love thee with mine eyes,
For they in thee a thousand errors note,
But 't is my heart that loves what they despise,
Who in despite of view is pleas'd to dote.
Nor are mine ears with thy tongue's tune delighted,
Nor tender feeling to base touches prone,
Nor taste, nor smell, desire to be invited
To any sensual feast with thee alone:
But my five wits, nor my five senses can
Dissuade one foolish heart from serving thee,
Who leaves unsway'd the likeness of a man,
Thy proud heart's slave and vassal wretch to be:
    Only my plague thus far I count my gain,
    That she that makes me sin, awards me pain.

142

Love is my sin, and thy dear virtue hate,
Hate of my sin, grounded on sinful loving,
O but with mine, compare thou thine own state,
And thou shalt find it merits not reproving,
Or if it do, not from those lips of thine,
That have profan'd their scarlet ornaments,
And seal'd false bonds of love as oft as mine,
Robb'd others' beds' revenues of their rents.
Be it lawful I love thee as thou lov'st those,
Whom thine eyes woo as mine importune thee,
Root pity in thy heart that when it grows,
Thy pity may deserve to pitied be.
    If thou dost seek to have what thou dost hide,
    By self-example mayst thou be denied.

143

Lo as a careful housewife runs to catch,
One of her feathered creatures broke away,
Sets down her babe and makes all swift despatch
In pursuit of the thing she would have stay:
Whilst her neglected child holds her in chase,
Cries to catch her whose busy care is bent,
To follow that which flies before her face,
Not prizing her poor infant's discontent;
So runn'st thou after that which flies from thee,
Whilst I thy babe chase thee afar behind,
But if thou catch thy hope turn back to me:
And play the mother's part, kiss me, be kind.
  So will I pray that thou mayst have thy Will,
  If thou turn back and my loud crying still.

144

Two loves I have of comfort and despair,
Which like two spirits do suggest me still,
The better angel is a man right fair:
The worser spirit a woman colour'd ill.
To win me soon to hell my female evil,
Tempteth my better angel from my side,
And would corrupt my saint to be a devil,
Wooing his purity with her foul pride.
And whether that my angel be turn'd fiend,
Suspect I may, yet not directly tell,
But being both from me both to each friend,
I guess one angel in another's hell.
  Yet this shall I ne'er know, but live in doubt,
  Till my bad angel fire my good one out.

145

Those lips that Love's own hand did make,
Breath'd forth the sound that said I hate,
To me that languish'd for her sake:
But when she saw my woeful state,
Straight in her heart did mercy come,
Chiding that tongue that ever sweet,
Was us'd in giving gentle doom:
And taught it thus anew to greet:
I hate she alter'd with an end,
That follow'd it as gentle day,
Doth follow night who like a fiend
From heaven to hell is flown away.
   I hate, from hate away she threw,
   And sav'd my life saying, not you.

146

Poor soul the centre of my sinful earth,
My sinful earth these rebel powers that thee array,
Why dost thou pine within and suffer dearth
Painting thy outward walls so costly gay?
Why so large cost having so short a lease,
Dost thou upon thy fading mansion spend?
Shall worms inheritors of this excess,
Eat up thy charge?   Is this thy body's end?
Then soul live thou upon thy servant's loss,
And let that pine to aggravate thy store;
Buy terms divine in selling hours of dross:
Within be fed, without be rich no more,
   So shalt thou feed on Death, that feeds on men,
   And Death once dead, there's no more dying then.

D

147

My love is as a fever longing still,
For that which longer nurseth the disease,
Feeding on that which doth preserve the ill,
Th' uncertain sickly appetite to please:
My reason the physician to my love,
Angry that his prescriptions are not kept
Hath left me, and I desperate now approve,
Desire is death, which physic did except.
Past cure I am, now reason is past care,
And frantic mad with evermore unrest,
My thoughts and my discourse as mad men's are,
At random from the truth vainly express'd.
　　For I have sworn thee fair, and thought thee bright,
　　Who art as black as hell, as dark as night.

148

O me! what eyes hath love put in my head,
Which have no correspondence with true sight,
Or if they have, where is my judgment fled,
That censures falsely what they see aright?
If that be fair whereon my false eyes dote,
What means the world to say it is not so?
If it be not, then love doth well denote,
Love's eye is not so true as all men's: no,
How can it? O how can love's eye be true,
That is so vex'd with watching and with tears?
No marvel then though I mistake my view,
The sun itself sees not, till heaven clears.
　　O cunning love, with tears thou keep'st me blind,
　　Lest eyes well seeing thy foul faults should find.

149

Canst thou O cruel, say I love thee not,
When I against myself with thee partake:
Do I not think on thee when I forgot
Am of myself, all tyrant for thy sake?
Who hateth thee that I do call my friend,
On whom frown'st thou that I do fawn upon,
Nay if thou lower'st on me do I not spend
Revenge upon myself with present moan?
What merit do I in myself respect,
That is so proud thy service to despise,
When all my best doth worship thy defect,
Commanded by the motion of thine eyes.
    But love hate on for now I know thy mind,
      Those that can see thou lov'st, and I am blind.

150

Oh from what power hast thou this powerful might,
With insufficiency my heart to sway,
To make me give the lie to my true sight,
And swear that brightness doth not grace the day?
Whence hast thou this becoming of things ill,
That in the very refuse of thy deeds,
There is such strength and warrantise of skill,
That in my mind thy worst all best exceeds?
Who taught thee how to make me love thee more,
The more I hear and see just cause of hate,
Oh though I love what others do abhor,
With others thou shouldst not abhor my state.
    If thy unworthiness rais'd love in me,
      More worthy I to be belov'd of thee.

151

Love is too young to know what conscience is,
Yet who knows not conscience is born of love,
Then gentle cheater urge not my amiss,
Lest guilty of my faults thy sweet self prove.
For thou betraying me, I do betray
My nobler part to my gross body's treason,
My soul doth tell my body that he may
Triumph in love, flesh stays no farther reason,
But rising at thy name doth point out thee,
As his triumphant prize, proud of this pride,
He is contented thy poor drudge to be
To stand in thy affairs, fall by thy side.
　　No want of conscience hold it that I call,
　　Her love, for whose dear love I rise and fall.

152

In loving thee thou know'st I am forsworn,
But thou art twice forsworn to me love swearing,
In act thy bed-vow broke and new faith torn,
In vowing new hate after new love bearing:
But why of two oaths' breach do I accuse thee,
When I break twenty: I am perjur'd most,
For all my vows are oaths but to misuse thee:
And all my honest faith in thee is lost.
For I have sworn deep oaths of thy deep kindness:
Oaths of thy love, thy truth, thy constancy,
And to enlighten thee gave eyes to blindness,
Or made them swear against the thing they see.
　　For I have sworn thee fair: more perjur'd I,
　　To swear against the truth so foul a lie.

153

Cupid laid by his brand and fell asleep,
A maid of Dian's this advantage found,
And his love-kindling fire did quickly steep
In a cold valley-fountain of that ground:
Which borrow'd from this holy fire of love,
A dateless lively heat still to endure,
And grew a seething bath which yet men prove,
Against strange maladies a sovereign cure:
But at my mistress' eye Love's brand new-fired,
The boy for trial needs would touch my breast,
I sick withal the help of bath desired,
And thither hied a sad distemper'd guest.
    But found no cure, the bath for my help lies,
    Where Cupid got new fire; my mistress' eyes.

154

The little Love-God lying once asleep,
Laid by his side his heart-inflaming brand,
Whilst many Nymphs that vow'd chaste life to keep,
Came tripping by, but in her maiden hand,
The fairest votary took up that fire,
Which many Legions of true hearts had warm'd,
And so the General of hot desire,
Was sleeping by a Virgin hand disarm'd.
This brand she quenched in a cool Well by,
Which from Love's fire took heat perpetual,
Growing a bath and healthful remedy,
For men diseas'd: but I my Mistress' thrall,
    Came there for cure and this by that I prove,
    Love's fire heats water, water cools not love.

FINIS

A Lover's Complaint

A LOVER'S COMPLAINT

by

WILLIAM SHAKESPEARE

From off a hill whose concave womb reworded,
A plaintful story from a sist'ring vale
My spirits t' attend this double voice accorded,
And down I laid to list the sad tun'd tale,
Ere long espied a fickle maid full pale
Tearing of papers, breaking rings a twain,
Storming her world with sorrows, wind and rain.

Upon her head a plaited hive of straw,
Which fortified her visage from the Sun,
Whereon the thought might think sometime it saw
The carcase of a beauty spent and done,
Time had not scythed all that youth begun,
Nor youth all quit, but spite of heaven's fell rage,
Some beauty peep'd, through lattice of sear'd age.

Oft did she heave her napkin to her eyne,
Which on it had conceited characters:
Laund'ring the silken figures in the brine,
That seasoned woe had pelleted in tears,
And often reading what contents it bears:
As often shrieking undistinguish'd woe,
In clamours of all size both high and low.

Sometimes her levell'd eyes their carriage ride,
As they did batt'ry to the spheres intend:
Sometimes diverted their poor balls are tied,
To th' orbed earth; sometimes they do extend,
Their view right on, anon their gazes lend,
To every place at once and no where fix'd,
The mind and sight distractedly commix'd.

Her hair nor loose nor tied in formal plait,
Proclaim'd in her a careless hand of pride;
For some untuck'd descended her sheav'd hat,
Hanging her pale and pined cheek beside,
Some in her threaden fillet still did bide,
And true to bondage would not break from thence,
Though slackly braided in loose negligence.

A thousand favours from a maund she drew,
Of amber crystal and of bedded jet,
Which one by one she in a river threw,
Upon whose weeping margent she was set,
Like usury applying wet to wet,
Or monarch's hands that lets not bounty fall,
Where want cries some, but where excess begs all.

Of folded schedules had she many a one,
Which she perus'd, sigh'd, tore and gave the flood,
Crack'd many a ring of posied gold and bone,
Bidding them find their sepulchres in mud,
Found yet mo letters sadly penn'd in blood,
With sleided silk, feat and affectedly
Enswath'd and seal'd to curious secrecy.

These often bath'd she in her fluxive eyes,
And often kiss'd, and often gave to tear,
Cried O false blood thou register of lies,
What unapproved witness dost thou bear!
Ink would have seem'd more black and damned here!
This said in top of rage the lines she rents,
Big discontent, so breaking their contents.

A reverend man that graz'd his cattle nigh,
Sometime a blusterer that the ruffle knew
Of Court of City, and had let go by
The swiftest hours observed as they flew,
Towards this afflicted fancy fastly drew:
And privileg'd by age desires to know
In brief the grounds and motives of her woe.

So slides he down upon his grained bat;
And comely distant sits he by her side,
When he again desires her, being sat,
Her grievance with his hearing to divide:
If that from him there may be ought applied
Which may her suffering ecstasy assuage
'Tis promis'd in the charity of age.

Father she says, though in me you behold,
The injury of many a blasting hour;
Let it not tell your judgment I am old,
Not age, but sorrow, over me hath power;
I might as yet have been a spreading flower
Fresh to myself, if I had self applied
Love to myself, and to no love beside.

But woe is me, too early I attended
A youthful suit it was to gain my grace;
O one by nature's outwards so commended,
That maidens' eyes stuck over all his face,
Love lack'd a dwelling and made him her place,
And when in his fair parts she did abide,
She was new lodg'd and newly deified.

His browny locks did hang in crooked curls,
And every light occasion of the wind
Upon his lips their silken parcels hurls,
What's sweet to do, to do will aptly find,
Each eye that saw him did enchant the mind:
For on his visage was in little drawn,
What largeness thinks in paradise was sawn.

Small show of man was yet upon his chin,
His phœnix down began but to appear
Like unshorn velvet, on that termless skin
Whose bare out-bragg'd the web it seem'd to wear.
Yet showed his visage by that cost more dear,
And nice affections wavering stood in doubt
If best were as it was, or best without.

His qualities were beauteous as his form,
For maiden-tongu'd he was and thereof free;
Yet if men mov'd him, was he such a storm
As oft twixt May and April is to see,
When winds breathe sweet, unruly though they be.
His rudeness so with his authoriz'd youth,
Did livery falseness in a pride of truth.

Well could he ride, and often men would say
That horse his mettle from his rider takes
Proud of subjection, noble by the sway,
What rounds, what bounds, what course, what stop he
    makes;
And controversy hence a question takes,
Whether the horse by him became his deed,
Or he his manage, by th' well doing steed.

But quickly on this side the verdict went,
His real habitude gave life and grace
To appertainings and to ornament,
Accomplish'd in himself not in his case:
All aids themselves made fairer by their place,
Can for additions, yet their purpos'd trim
Piec'd not his grace but were all grac'd by him.

So on the tip of his subduing tongue
All kind of arguments and question deep,
All replication prompt, and reason strong
For his advantage still did wake and sleep,
To make the weeper laugh, the laughter weep,
He had the dialect and different skill,
Catching all passions in his craft of will.

That he did in the general bosom reign
Of young, of old, and sexes both enchanted,
To dwell with him in thoughts, or to remain
In personal duty, following where he haunted,
Consent's bewitch'd, ere he desire have granted,
And dialogu'd for him what he would say,
Ask'd their own wills and made their wills obey.

Many there were that did his picture get
To serve their eyes, and in it put their mind,
Like fools that in th' imagination set
The goodly objects which abroad they find
Of lands and mansions, theirs in thought assign'd,
And labouring in mo pleasures to bestow them,
Than the true gouty landlord which doth owe them.

So many have that never touch'd his hand
Sweetly suppos'd them mistress of his heart:
My woeful self that did in freedom stand,
And was my own fee simple (not in part)
What with his art in youth and youth in art
Threw my affections in his charmed power,
Reserv'd the stalk and gave him all my flower.

Yet did I not as some my equals did
Demand of him, nor being desired yielded,
Finding myself in honour so forbid,
With safest distance I mine honour shielded,
Experience for me many bulwarks builded
Of proofs new bleeding which remain'd the foil
Of this false jewel, and his amorous spoil.

But ah who ever shunn'd by precedent,
The destin'd ill she must herself assay,
Or forc'd examples 'gainst her own content
To put the by-past perils in her way?
Counsel may stop a while what will not stay:
For when we rage, advice is often seen
By blunting us to make our wits more keen.

Nor gives it satisfaction to our blood,
That we must curb it upon others' proof,
To be forbid the sweets that seems so good,
For fear of harms that preach in our behoof;
O appetite from judgment stand aloof!
The one a palate hath that needs will taste,
Though reason weep and cry it is thy last.

For further I could say this man's untrue,
And knew the patterns of his foul beguiling,
Heard where his plants in others' orchards grew,
Saw how deceits were gilded in his smiling,
Knew vows were ever brokers to defiling,
Thought characters and words merely but art,
And bastards of his foul adulterate heart.

And long upon these terms I held my City,
Till thus he gan besiege me : Gentle maid,
Have of my suffering youth some feeling pity
And be not of my holy vows afraid,
That's to ye sworn to none was ever said,
For feasts of love I have been call'd unto
Till now did ne'er invite nor never vow.

All my offences that abroad you see
Are errors of the blood none of the mind:
Love made them not, with acture they may be,
Where neither party is nor true nor kind,
They sought their shame that so their shame did find,
And so much less of shame in me remains,
By how much of me their reproach contains.

Among the many that mine eyes have seen,
Not one whose flame my heart so much as warmed,
Or my affection put to th' smallest teen,
Or any of my leisures ever charmed,
Harm have I done to them but ne'er was harmed,
·Kept hearts in liveries, but mine own was free,
And reign'd commanding in his monarchy.

Look here what tributes wounded fancies sent me,
Of paled pearls and rubies red as blood:
Figuring that they their passions likewise lent me
Of grief and blushes, aptly understood
In bloodless white, and the encrimson'd mood,
Effects of terror and dear modesty,
Encamp'd in hearts but fighting outwardly.

And lo behold these talents of their hair,
With twisted metal amorously empleach'd
I have receiv'd from many a several fair,
Their kind acceptance, weepingly beseech'd,
With th' annexions of fair gems enrich'd,
And deep brain'd sonnets that did amplify
Each stone's dear Nature, worth and quality.

The diamond? why 'twas beautiful and hard,
Whereto his invis'd properties did tend,
The deep green em'rald in whose fresh regard,
Weak sights their sickly radiance do amend,
The heaven hu'd sapphire and the opal blend
With objects manifold; each several stone,
With wit well blazon'd smil'd or made some moan.

Lo all these trophies of affections hot,
Of pensiv'd and subdu'd desires the tender,
Nature hath charg'd me that I hoard them not,
But yield them up where I myself must render:
That is to you my origin and ender:
For these of force must your oblations be,
Since I their altar, you enpatron me.

Oh then advance (of yours) that phraseless hand,
Whose white weighs down the airy scale of praise,
Take all these similes to your own command,
Hallowed with sighs that burning lungs did raise:
What me your minister for you obeys
Works under you, and to your audit comes
Their distract parcels, in combined sums.

Lo this device was sent me from a Nun,
Or Sister sanctified of holiest note,
Which late her noble suit in court did shun,
Whose rarest havings made the blossoms dote,
For she was sought by spirits of richest coat,
But kept cold distance, and did thence remove,
To spend her living in eternal love.

But oh my sweet what labour is 't to leave,
The thing we have not, mast'ring what not strives,
Playing the place which did no form receive,
Playing patient sports in unconstrain'd gyves,
She that her fame so to herself contrives,
The scars of battle 'scapeth by the flight,
And makes her absence valiant, not her might.

Oh pardon me in that my boast is true,
The accident which brought me to her eye,
Upon the moment did her force subdue,
And now she would the caged cloister fly:
Religious love put out religion's eye:
Not to be tempted would she be enur'd,
And now to tempt all liberty procur'd.

How mighty then you are, Oh hear me tell,
The broken bosoms that to me belong,
Have emptied all their fountains in my well:
And mine I pour your Ocean all among:
I strong o'er them and you o'er me being strong,
Must for your victory us all congest,
As compound love to physic your cold breast.

My parts had power to charm a sacred Sun,
Who disciplin'd I dieted in grace,
Believ'd her eyes, when they t' assail begun,
All vows and consecrations giving place:
O most potential love, vow, bond, nor space
In thee hath neither sting, knot, nor confine
For thou art all and all things else are thine.

When thou impressest what are precepts worth
Of stale example? when thou wilt inflame,
How coldly those impediments stand forth
Of wealth, of filial fear, law, kindred fame,
Love's arms are peace, 'gainst rule, 'gainst sense, 'gainst
    shame
And sweetens in the suff'ring pangs it bears,
The aloes of all forces, shocks and fears.

Now all these hearts that do on mine depend,
Feeling it break, with bleeding groans they pine,
And supplicant their sighs to you extend
To leave the batt'ry that you make 'gainst mine,
Lending soft audience, to my sweet design,
And credent soul, to that strong bonded oath,
That shall prefer and undertake my troth.

This said, his wat'ry eyes he did dismount,
Whose sights till then were levell'd on my face,
Each cheek a river running from a fount,
With brinish current downward flowed a pace:
Oh how the channel to the stream gave grace!
Who glaz'd with crystal gate the glowing roses,
That flame through water which their hue incloses.

Oh father, what a hell of witch-craft lies,
In the small orb of one particular tear?
But with the inundation of the eyes,
What rocky heart to water will not wear?
What breast so cold that is not warmed here,
Or cleft effect, cold modesty hot wrath:
Both fire from hence, and chill extincture hath.

For lo his passion but an art of craft,
Even there resolv'd my reason into tears,
There my white stole of chastity I daft,
Shook off my sober guards, and civil fears,
Appear to him as he to me appears:
All melting, though our drops this diff'rence bore,
His poison'd me, and mine did him restore.

In him a plenitude of subtle matter,
Applied to cautels, all strange forms receives,
Of burning blushes, or of weeping water,
Or sounding paleness : and he takes and leaves,
In either's aptness as it best deceives :
To blush at speeches rank, to weep at woes
Or to turn white and sound at tragic shows.

That not a heart which in his level came,
Could 'scape the hail of his all hurting aim,
Showing fair Nature is both kind and tame :
And veil'd in them did win whom he would maim,
Against the thing he sought, he would exclaim,
When he most burnt in heart-wish'd luxury,
He preach'd pure maid, and prais'd cold chastity.

Thus merely with the garment of a grace,
The naked and concealed fiend he cover'd,
That th' unexperient gave the tempter place,
Which like a cherubin above them hover'd,
Who young and simple would not be so lover'd.
Ay me I fell, and yet do question make,
What I should do again for such a sake.

O that infected moisture of his eye,
O that false fire which in his cheek so glow'd :
O that forc'd thunder from his heart did fly,
O that sad breath his spungy lungs bestowed,
O all that borrowed motion seeming owed,
Would yet again betray the sore-betrayed,
And new pervert a reconciled Maid.

FINIS

NOTES TO THE SONNETS

*References to the text are to the number and line
of each Sonnet*

Dedication	Many guesses at the identity of 'Mr W. H.' have been made, of which the more interesting are:–

(a) *William Hall.* Sir Sidney Lee noted that an edition of the *Fourfold Meditations* of Fr Robert Southwell, the Jesuit martyr, printed 1606, was dedicated 'To the Right Worshipful and Vertuous Gentleman, Matthew Saunders, Esquire. W. H. wisheth, with long life, a prosperous achievement of his good desires'. Lee identified this W. H. with the W. H. of the Sonnets and declared that the original was one William Hall, a printer in a small way. This identification has been accepted by many. Beyond the fact that Hall's initials were W. H. there is no other evidence to connect him with either publication, nor is it likely that he would have commended the work of a Jesuit martyr, for he printed anti-Catholic books.

(b) *Sir William Harvey,* who married the Earl of Southampton's mother in 1598; a likely person to have access to the original manuscript. He has also a greater claim to be the W. H. of Father Southwell's *Fourfold Meditations,* for the Southampton family was strongly Catholic. He might also have been the 'onlie begetter' in the sense that he first suggested that Shakespeare should address Southampton.

(c) *William Herbert,* Earl of Pembroke.

I L. 2	*beauty's rose:* a common figure for youthful beauty. Hotspur speaks of Richard the Second as 'that sweet lovely rose'.
L. 6	*self substantial fuel:* fuel of your own substance.

1 LL. 11–12	*Within thine own ... niggarding:*	instead of expanding to blossom and seed you contract and come to nothing. *Content:* that which contains, substance.
2 L. 1	*forty winters:*	In Shakespeare's time men matured, married and died earlier than to-day.
L. 4	*totter'd:*	tattered.
L. 11	*sum my count:*	audit my account with Nature.
L. 11	*old excuse:*	justification in old age.
4 L. 3	*Nature's bequest gives nothing:*	the beauty which Nature has bestowed is a loan to be passed on.
5		'Time destroys the summer flowers, but the essence of flowers distilled lives on as a remembrance of summer.'
5 L. 14	*Leese:*	lose.
7 L. 1	*gracious light:*	the Sun.
9 L. 4	*makeless:*	mateless.
11 L. 9	*for store:*	for increasing the stock.
12 L. 4	*sable:*	black.
L. 14	*breed to brave him:*	posterity which defies Time when the sire is gone.
13 L. 6	*determination:*	end.
L. 10	*husbandry:*	household management.
14 L. 2	*Astronomy:*	astrology. Astrologers, in their humble capacity as almanack makers, added to the penny Calendar a forecast of the weather for the year as well as prognostications of higher events.
L. 14	*Thy end is Truth's ...:*	When you die, Truth and Beauty die with you.
15 L. 12	*sullied:*	smirched.
16 L. 8	*painted counterfeit:*	portrait.
17 L. 12	*stretched metre:*	poetic licence.
20 L. 2	*passion:*	fervent declaration of love.
L. 6	*Gilding:*	as the Sun's light gilds.
L. 7	*A man in hue ... controlling:*	'A man in appearance surpassing all others.' The Quarto prints 'A man in hew all *Hews,* in his controwling' (see Introduction p. 21) which may point to a pun.

21 L. 1	*Muse:* poet.
L. 2	*Stirr'd by:* inspired by.
L. 8	*rondure:* round.
22 L. 4	*expiate:* end.
23 L. 5	*for fear of trust:* fearing to trust myself to speak.
L. 10	*presagers:* interpreters.
24 L. 1	*steel'd:* engraved.
L. 2	*table:* tablet, notebook.
25 LL. 9–11	*The painful warrior ... worth ... forth:* The Quarto reads 'quite' in line 11. Rhyme demands either 'forth' in line 11 or 'fight' in line 9.
L. 9	*painful:* laborious.
L. 10	*foil'd:* defeated.
26	This Sonnet reads like a verse paraphrase of the Dedication to *Lucrece* (see p. 20). If so, it probably accompanied the copy of the poem sent to Southampton.
28 L. 12	*twire:* peep.
29 L. 7	*scope:* opportunity.
30 L. 6	*dateless:* endless.
31	'My absence from you reminds me of all my friends lost: you have all their precious qualities.'
31 L. 1	*endeared:* made more precious.
32 L. 11	*dearer birth:* more valuable offering.
33 L. 4	*alchymy:* the alchemist's quest was how to turn base metal to gold.
L. 6	*rack:* cloud drift.
34 L. 12	*cross:* burden, sorrow.
35 L. 4	*canker:* maggot.
L. 6	*Authorising thy trespass ... compare:* allowing your offence by comparing it with others' faults.
L. 7	*salving:* soothing.
36 L. 6	*separable spite:* a spite which separates.
L. 10	*my bewailed guilt:* Nothing is known of the event to which this refers.
37 L. 3	*dearest spite:* bitterest spite.
L. 7	*Entitled:* enrolled.

38 L. 8   *give invention light:* give light to inspiration.

L. 12   *Eternal numbers:* immortal verse.

L. 13   *curious:* particular, censorious.

39 LL. 1–2   *Oh how ... me?:* How can I praise with modesty
             when you are the better part of myself?

40–42   In these three sonnets the poet laments the loss of
             his mistress and takes what consolation he can. It
             is likely that the mistress is the same as the woman
             addressed in the last series. Sonnets 133, 134, 144
             tell essentially the same story.

43 L. 12   *sightless:* blind.

44 L. 1   *If the dull substance ... thought:* If my body were not
             material I would come to you quick as thought.

45   In this Sonnet Shakespeare carries on from 44 the
             idea of the four elements of air, fire, earth, water.

45 L. 1   *purging fire:* fire is essentially a purifying agent.

L. 7   *with two alone:* i.e. when the volatile elements of air
             and fire are subtracted there remains only the
             heavy elements, earth and water.

L. 9   *life's composition be recured:* until the four be re-
             assembled.

46 L. 2   *conquest of thy sight:* booty won by seeing you.

L. 10   *quest:* jury.

L. 12   *moiety:* share.

48 L. 14   *For truth proves thievish ...:* Even Truth would
             become a thief for such a prize.

49 L. 8   *settled gravity:* sober respectability forbids friendship
             with a player.

L. 9   *ensconce:* shelter.

52 L. 8   *captain:* principal.

53 L. 5   *counterfeit:* picture.

L. 9   *foizon:* increase.

54 L. 5   *canker-blooms:* blossoms of the wild rose.

L. 14   *vade:* fade.

55 L. 9   *all-oblivious enmity:* oblivion that is enemy to all things.

L. 13   *till the judgment ... arise:* until you rise again at the
             Day of Judgment.

58 L. 9   *charter*: privilege to do what you please.

59 L. 8   *character*: handwriting.

    L. 11   *Whether*: pronounced as a monosyllable 'where'.

62 L. 10   *chopp'd*: chapped, rough.

    L. 13   *'T is thee ... praise*: By identifying myself with you, I fancy myself beautiful.

63 L. 1   *Against*: against the time when.

66 L. 3   *needy Nothing ... jollity*: the natural beggar gaily dressed – the antithesis to the previous line.

    L. 11   *Simplicity*: foolishness.

67   'Why should he live amidst such general corruption? So that Nature may see what perfection once was.'

67 L. 4   *lace*: ornament.

    L. 8   *Roses of shadow*: painted roses.

68   'So his beauty is a pattern of the ancient beauty' before painting and false hair imitated true beauty.

68 L. 1   *map of days out-worn*: picture of days past.

    L. 3   *fair*: beauty.

    L. 5   *golden tresses of the dead*: The wigmaker obtained his hair where he could, often from the heads of corpses.

69 L. 3   *due*: the Quarto reads 'end'.

    L. 14   *The soil ... grow*: The Quarto reads 'solye'. The blemish is because you grow too familiar with inferiors.

70 L. 3   *The ornament ... suspect*: Beauty is always suspected.

    L. 12   *envy, evermore enlarg'd*: envy is always at liberty.

76 L. 6   *And keep invention ... weed*: and express my thoughts always in the same style. *Weed*: garment.

77   Sent with the present of a notebook.

79 L. 5   *lovely argument*: the subject of thy loveliness.

80 L. 2   *better spirit doth use your name*: see note on Sonnet 86.

82 L. 1   *married*: irrevocably tied.

    L. 2   *attaint*: blame.

    L. 11   *sympathis'd*: feelingly expressed.

83 L. 1   *painting*: superfluous ornament.
   L. 4   *tender*: offer.
   L. 7   *modern*: commonplace.
85 L. 4   *fil'd*: polished. Francis Meres in praising Shakespeare's plays wrote that 'the Muses would speak with Shakespeare's fine filed phrase, if they would speak English'.
86   The rival poet of whom Shakespeare was jealous is variously identified: George Chapman is likeliest. 'It is bound to remind students of the peculiarities of Chapman: (1) The gorgeous and rather overdressed quality of his really "great verse"; (2) His belief in spirits, or, at any rate, telepathy, indicated in the dedication and the opening lines of his portion of *Hero and Leander*; (3) His sometimes inhuman rhodomontades and obscurity, – writing "above a mortal pitch"; (4) The special cult of night in his early poems; (5) His extravagant dedications of poems and even plays to persons of rank; witness that of the early books of his Homer to Essex.' [*Shakespeare's Sonnets*. Ed. Tucker Brooke.]
87 L. 8   *patent ... swerving*: my grant of love lapses.
   L. 11   *misprision*: mistaking.
88 L. 1   *set me light*: slightly value me.
91 L. 5   *humour*: peculiarity.
98 L. 4   *heavy Saturn*: Those born under Saturn were heavy and melancholic.
100 L. 11   *a satire to decay*: if there are any wrinkles they will mock decay.
102 L. 8   *Philomel in summer's front*: the nightingale in early summer.
104   The friendship has lasted three years. 'Since he first met his correspondent three periods of time had elapsed, in each of which a spring had preceded an autumn (l. 5) and a summer a winter (ll. 3 and 4) while three periods each containing

an April, a May and a June (l. 7) were also included
in the three-year period which he is describing.
However the reader varies the arrangement of the
seasons mentioned, he will find that he can arrange
them in one way only if he is to observe all the
conditions laid down by the poet, i.e. he must
place his first meeting with his friend in the spring,
indeed in the April of some year, and he must date
the sonnet as having been written at the end of
winter (or very soon after that) just three years
after the first eventful interview between the two
men.' [J. A. Fort. *A Time Scheme for Shakespeare's
Sonnets.*] Fort further argued that the likeliest April
for the beginning of the period was 1593 when
Shakespeare dedicated *Venus and Adonis* to
Southampton.

106 L. 5 *blazon*: description.

107 This Sonnet so obviously refers to current events
that it should provide a date. Unfortunately, like
the others, it is ambiguous. The 'mortal Moon' is
Queen Elizabeth, but it is doubtful whether 'her
eclipse endur'd' means 'has been blotted out'
[i.e. she is dead], or 'has passed through a period
of eclipse', [i.e. she has survived]. Two dates are
reasonable:

(*a*) Spring 1603. This date fits all the references.
Queen Elizabeth died on 24th March. Southamp-
ton was a prisoner in the Tower during the
Queen's life ['forfeit to a confin'd doom']. It
was very generally expected that on the Queen's
death civil war and anarchy would follow; but
the prophets of disaster were proved wrong, for
James I succeeded without opposition and was
enthusiastically welcomed. One of his first acts
was to release Southampton. If the Sonnet was
written in the Spring of 1603 it is an additional
argument for identifying the Youth with South-

ampton. On the other hand it seems unlikely that there should have been an interval of seven years between 104 and 107, and of ten years since the series began.

(b) Autumn 1596. On 6th September 1596 Queen Elizabeth emerged from the period of her 'grand Climacteric', her 63rd year. The climacteric periods – each seventh year – were regarded as crises in human life and the 8th, 9th and 10th climacteric of Queen Elizabeth were all decisive. In the 8th the Armada came and was defeated; in the 9th the Spaniards captured Calais and disaster seemed imminent; in the 10th she died. Prophets of disaster were very busy in 1596. In the Spring the Bishop of St David's even preached a sermon before the Queen on mystical numbers and the grand climacteric, and devised a prayer for the Queen to offer in which she was made to say 'O Lord, I am now entered a good way into the climacterical year of mine age which mine enemies wish and hope to be fatal to me'. The gloomy prophets were however confounded in the summer. In August a brilliant victory was won over the Spaniards at Cadiz which was sacked and burned, the alliance with France was renewed, and in the early autumn there was a general feeling of optimism.

109 L. 2	*qualify:*	moderate.
L. 5	*rang'd:*	wandered.
110 L. 2	*motley:*	clown.
L. 7	*blenches:*	glances aside.
111 L. 4	*public means:*	i.e. as an entertainer.
L. 10	*eysell:*	vinegar, regarded as a protective medicine against the plague.
112 L. 4	*o'er-green:*	as grass over a bare patch.
L. 8	*steel'd sense:*	feelings firm as steel.
LL. 10–11	*adder's sense ... stopped:*	The wicked are 'like the

deaf adder that stoppeth her ear, which will
not hearken to the voice of the charmers, charming
never so wisely'. Psalm 58, v. 4.

113 L. 6   *latch*: lay hold of. The Quarto reads *lack*.

114 L. 8   *beams*: eye-beams, the eye being supposed to shoot
out beams of sight.

L. 11   *gust*: taste.

115 L. 1   *Those lines ... do lie*: The thought of this sonnet
resembles Donne's poem *Love's Growth*.

       Methinks I lied all winter, when I swore

       My love was infinite, when spring makes it
more.

116 L. 5   *mark*: sea mark, a conspicuous object by which
seamen check their course.

L. 8   *height be taken*: i.e. in reckoning a ship's position by
the stars.

117 L. 9   *Book*: enter as a debit.

118 L. 12   *rank*: overfull.

121 L. 11   *bevel*: slanting.

122 L. 1   *tables*: notebooks.

L. 2   *character'd*: written.

L. 10   *tallies*: a tally was a stick on which notches were cut
to record amounts due.

123 L. 4   *dressings of a former sight*: new forms of old sights.

124 L. 1   *love ... child of state*: If my love was merely born of
policy, it would die when love was no longer
profitable.

L. 7   *thralled discontent*: discontent held in subjection.

L. 14   *Which die for goodness ... crime*: who when executed
for crime protest that they are martyrs for a good
cause. Shakespeare is thinking of some political or
religious conspiracy, but the reference is too vague,
and conspiracies were too common for it to be
identified.

125 L. 1   *bore the canopy*: On ceremonial occasions a canopy
was often carried over the Sovereign.

126   With this Sonnet the series to the Youth ends.

The Quarto prints empty brackets (retained in the text) to indicate missing lines. The poem however is not a formal sonnet of 14 lines but rather an Envoy, or Conclusion.

126 L. 12 *quietus*: receipt, formal acknowledgment of payment.

L. 32 *render*: give up.

127 This is the first of the Sonnets to the Dark Woman. 'There have been several claimants to the dubious distinction of being the "Dark Lady". The tone of Shakespeare's Sonnets to her suggests that she was not a person of any position, and there is scattered evidence that in the 1590's one of the well-known courtesans was notoriously dark. In the Gray's Inn Revels, amongst those brought in to pay mock homage to the Prince of Purpool "*Lucy Negro*, Abbess *de Clerkenwell*, holdeth the Nunnery of *Clerkenwell*, with the Lands and Priviledges thereunto belonging, of the Prince of *Purpoole* by Night-Service in *Cauda*, and to find a Choir of Nuns, with burning Lamps, to chaunt *Placebo* to the Gentlemen of the Prince's Privy-Chamber, on the Day of His Excellency's Coronation." (Malone Soc. Reprint, p. 12.) This "Lucy Negro" I would very tentatively identify as the Dark Lady. In Guilpin's *Skialetheia*, 1598, Epigrams 57, 61 and 62 are to a light lady called Nigrina. Both Southampton and Guilpin were members of Gray's Inn. In Weever's *Epigrams*, 1599, Third Week, Epig. 12, are verses *In Byrrham*:

Is *Byrrha* brown? Who doth the question aske?
Her face is pure as Ebonie ieat blacke,
It's hard to know her face from her fair maske,
Beautie in her seemes beautie still to lacke,
Nay, she's snow-white, but for that russet skin,
Which like a vaile doth keep her whiteness in.'

[*Shakespeare at Work*, p. 310.]

127 L. 1   *fair:* beautiful.

    L. 3   *successive heir:* next in descent.

    L. 5   *put on Nature's power:* i.e. by painting improve on Nature.

128 L. 5   *jacks:* keys.

130 L. 5   *damask'd:* adorned.

133 L. 6   *my friend and me:* The echo of Sonnets 40–2.

    L. 6   *engrossed:* monopolized.

134 L. 9   *statute:* legal security.

135   The italics of the Quarto, emphasizing the pun on 'will' and 'Will' are kept.

135 L. 5   *will:* desire.

137 L. 9   *several:* separate.

144 L. 2   *suggest:* urge.

146 L. 2   The printer of the Quarto has unfortunately repeated 'My sinful earth' instead of the right word which editors variously guess. Some such word as 'Bearing' or 'Feeding' is required.

153   This and the next Sonnet have nothing to do with the series. They are adaptations of Greek epigrams.

153 L. 7   *a seething bath:* probably a reference to Bath, which was as famous in Shakespeare's as in Roman times.

NOTES TO A LOVER'S COMPLAINT

P. 104 L. 1   *reworded:* echoed.

    L. 15   *eyne:* eyes.

    L. 16   *conceited characters:* elaborate devices.

    L. 18   *seasoned:* salt.

    L. 18   *pelleted:* dropped.

    L. 20   *undistinguish'd:* inarticulate.

P. 105 L. 1   *levell'd eyes their carriage ride:* her eyes are aimed, like a cannon on its carriage, against the stars.

L. 11 *pined:* thin.

L. 15 *maund:* basket.

L. 24 *posied gold:* Lovers' rings were often inscribed with a posy or little motto.

L. 26 *sleided silk:* sleeve silk, i.e. some strands of natural silk, often used for tying personal letters.

L. 26 *feat:* neat.

P. 106 L. 1 *fluxive:* flowing.

L. 9 *ruffle:* tumult.

L. 12 *fancy:* love, lover.

L. 15 *bat:* staff.

L. 20 *ecstasy:* emotion.

P. 107 L. 14 *What largeness thinks in paradise was sawn:* A corrupt line, of which the true reading can only be guessed. *Sawn:* (perhaps)=seen.

L. 16 *phoenix down:* it is not clear why the youthful lip should be called 'phoenix', unless as a far-fetched conceit for 'rare', 'incomparable'.

L. 17 *termless:* youthful.

L. 18 *bare:* bareness.

P. 108 L. 7 *manage:* horsemanship.

L. 17 *replication:* retort.

P. 109 L. 11 *fee simple:* absolute possession.

L. 20 *foil:* setting.

P. 110 L. 12 *brokers:* agents. As Polonius puts it, giving similar advice to Ophelia,

> In few, Ophelia,
> Do not believe his vows, for they are brokers,
> Not of that dye which their investments show,
> But mere implorators of unholy suits.

P. 110 L. 24 *acture:* act.

P. 111 L. 3 *teen:* sorrow.

L. 6 *in liveries:* as servants.

L. 15 *talents of their hair:* offerings of their hair.

L. 16 *empleach'd:* intertwined.

L. 23 *invis'd:* unseen.

L. 28 *blazon'd:* painted.

P. 112 L. 14 *distract parcels:* separate items.

L. 19 *richest coat:* i.e. noblemen with illustrious coats of arms.

L. 24 *playing the place:* the word 'playing' is repeated from l. 25 in place of some word meaning 'flying' or the like.

L. 25 *unconstrain'd gyves:* fetters which do not restrain.

P. 113 L. 6 *enur'd:* accustomed.

L. 28 *aloes:* bitterness.

P. 114 L. 13 *Who glaz'd ... incloses:* His cheeks, covered with tears, look like roses covered with crystals.

L. 20 *cleft effect:* divided into two.

L. 24 *daft:* took off.

P. 115 L. 2 *cautels:* craftiness, treacheries.

L. 7 *sound:* swoon.

L. 8 *level:* aim.

L. 13 *luxury:* lust.

L. 28 *reconciled:* an absolved penitent.

★